# DIS(
# AVIATION TRAILS

Paul Shaw

Midland Publishing Limited

# CONTENTS

For Artie and Till

© 1996 Paul Shaw
ISBN 1 85780 049 4

Published by
Midland Publishing Limited
24 The Hollow, Earl Shilton
Leicester, LE9 7NA, England

Design concept and layout
© Midland Publishing Limited and
Stephen Thompson Associates
Edited by Ken Ellis

Printed in England by
Woolnough Bookbinding Limited
Irthlingborough, Northamptonshire

Title Page Illustration:
*Memorial to the 401st BG at Deenethorpe.
Alas, the control tower in the background is
no more.* Paul Shaw

# INTRODUCTION

The aim of this guide is to direct those unfamiliar with an area to some of the places of aviation interest that it has to offer. It will help readers to make the most of a day out where more can be seen, no time is lost, fuel is saved, frustration is avoided, pitfalls revealed; all adding up to a more enjoyable day. Distances and times are given enabling readers to pace the day and give a feel of the compactness of each tour. They will also help if one wishes to spend longer at one venue and leave out others. Route notes are brief, but contain those important items that will help keep one on track, even if blown off course!

The motivation for compiling this guide came from my own experiences. My work takes me off the main routes of my local area. These occasions have given rise to many discoveries I may not have otherwise made. I packaged these discoveries into an airfield coach tour that was successful and was enjoyed by many knowledgeable people. Because of their appetite for these tours and my enjoyment of presenting them, I have had to purposely research and reconnoitre areas unknown to me. The biggest surprise of the day for me was the number of people who said, 'I've passed so close to here many times and never knew this was here'. I have gone on to organise many other tours of different areas for an appreciative audience.

This is a book I wanted to buy myself, but because it was not on a shelf for me to acquire, I have written it for others. I enjoy people telling me exciting snippets of information that send me rushing off to look for myself, so please, spoil me and write and tell me of any you know. They will give me fresh ideas of where to visit and should you wish me to write another guide, I can pass on your knowledge to others, so we may all benefit (Correspondence to 24, The Hollow, Earl Shilton, Leicester, LE9 7NA.)

Paul Shaw
June 1996

## Acknowledgements:

Mike Bailey, Rosalyn Blackmore, Margaret Byard, Ron Clarke, Alan Curry, Pam Ellis, Aldon P Ferguson, Chris Haynes, Helen and James Males, Roger Richards, Dave Smith, Hugh Trevor, M Unwin, Jock Whitehouse.

And to those who contributed photographs, who are credited with their work.

Mary Denton drew the maps.

And to Sue and Michael.

## HOW TO USE THIS GUIDE

### SCOPE AND AIM

This book presents a series of suggestions of what might be seen on a tour of a particular area. It has been compiled with the best information available to the author at the time of going to press and every effort has been made to be as accurate as possible. However, neither the author nor Midland Publishing Limited can be held responsible for any errors or changes that may occur in the descriptions of each tour. Clearly, the situation at individual sites will change, eg buildings demolished, road numbers changed, museums close to the public etc. As regards museums etc, readers are urged to check details ahead with the museum involved and/or with the local tourist information centre and telephone numbers have been supplied to assist in this.

Each tour is designed to provide a comprehensive 'taste' of aeronautical venues within the area concerned, but this need not necessarily be a complete view of what is available in any one area. At no stage are the author or the publishers making recommendations about any of the venues mentioned. The aim is to highlight such places to the reader and let him/her come to their own conclusions.

### THE TRAILS

In general, each trail follows the same format. The main differences from this are Cornwall (Trail A) with is a linear trail and is centred upon Newquay, allowing 'sections' to be toured and Greater London (Trail E) which is best accomplished on foot and using public transport.

Each trail starts with a map. The map is designed to provide an overview of each trail and is not for navigation purposes. It is assumed that readers will arm themselves with a good touring road map for the purpose of following the trails. The map names major towns and roads. Individual venues are given by numbers which are decoded underneath the map. The numbers relate to the order in which the venues are taken in the tour.

Note that it is perfectly possible to start the tour at any of the venues given and then follow the loop around. The 'starting point' of the tour is a suggestion only and starting at another point (perhaps a more convenient place in relation to your point of arrival) will not affect the progression of the trail.

There follows a general, and deliberately personal, narrative on the nature and qualities of the tour in question. Highlights will vary from reader to reader, but it is thought important to convey a likelihood of the 'taste' of the overall trail.

Venues are then described in the order as given numerically on the map at the beginning of the section. Following the heading comes a mileage and time assessment. The mileage quoted is the approximate distance from the last venue to the present one. The time given is by way of broad indication only and is given to help readers plan their way around the trail. Clearly, average speeds and traffic conditions will vary considerably, but the time given has been deliberately made 'leisurely' as that is one of the aims of the day out!

How long readers will want to spend at each venue is, of course, very much up to them, and that will reflect their tastes and what is happening on the day.

Each of the trails (bearing in mind the differences within Trails A and E already mentioned) can be extended to a full weekend, with more time being taken at each one, and of course there are 'Diversions' on offer as well – see opposite page.

Following the mileage and time estimations come directions from one venue to another, given in bold, italic type. In most of the cases, these should provide no problem for readers, but it must be stressed that with some country lanes it will be a case of 'there is more than one way to skin a cat' and anyway, reader may well wish to experiment with other routes to the next venue.

The mention of a venue in this work does not indicate, or imply, right of access. In many cases, the items mentioned are on private land and the view will be from public roads and footpaths only. Adherence to both the highway and country codes and employment of common sense and courtesies are vital to those undertaking aviation trails! Some venues may well be available to closer inspection by prior appointment, and where this is believed to be the case, it is noted.

Much can be seen from public roads and footpaths and there is equally much satisfaction to be had from discovering the layout of an airfield from such vantage points.

Narrative for each venue will include a description of what is to be found today, including, where appropriate current aeronautical usage. Within the description of a venue will frequently be details of how to travel around an aerodrome and items of interest along the way. Again, many readers will want to make their own way around, as things unfold in front of them.

At the end of a venue's description, the new heading will appear and directions concerning how to get there will be given in what will quickly become an established, repeating pattern.

At the end of each trail, directions are given back to the start point, but again it may well be that readers who have started at another part of the 'circle' will continue on anyway, or others may see this point as a suitable place to find a road home.

## 'DIVERSIONS'

Most of the trails will also offer extension, or 'diversions', sometimes quite local, others at a distance. It must be remembered that these are extra to the trail and will consume more time, or make the day more crowded. Local diversions are not given a major heading and can be taken as not consuming much in the way of miles, or time.

More sweeping diversions often are given by way of including airfields close by, but not directly within the theme of the trail. In these cases, they are given major headings, plus italicised directions. Readers must note that the distances and times quotes for these diversions are *one way only* and that the time needed to be allocated to them will need careful planning. In most cases, directions are given to resume the trail at the next venue, but it may well be that readers will want to plough their own route onwards, perhaps changing the order of venues.

# BIBLIOGRAPHY

*Action Stations 1, Military Airfields of East Anglia*, 2nd Edition, Michael J F Bowyer, Patrick Stephens, Wellingborough, 1990.

*Action Stations 2, Military Airfields of Lincolnshire and the East Midlands*, Bruce Barrymore Halpenny, Patrick Stephens, Cambridge, 1981.

*Action Stations 3, Military Airfields of Wales and the North-West*, 2nd Edition, David J Smith, Patrick Stephens, Wellingborough, 1991.

*Action Stations 4, Military Airfields of Yorkshire,* Bruce Barrymore Halpenny, Patrick Stephens, Cambridge, 1982.

*Action Stations 5, Military Airfields of the South-West*, 2nd Edition, Chris Ashworth, Patrick Stephens, Wellingborough, 1990.

*Action Stations 6, Military Airfields of the Cotswolds and the Central Midlands*, 2nd Edition, Michael J F Bowyer, Patrick Stephens, Wellingborough, 1990.

*Action Stations 7, Military Airfields of Scotland, the North-East and Northern Ireland,* David J Smith, Patrick Stephens, Cambridge, 1983.

*Aeronautical Memorials of Norfolk*, Huby Fairhead, Norfolk & Suffolk Aviation Museum, Flixton, 1989.

*Air Force Memorials of Lincolnshire*, Mike Ingham, Midland Publishing Ltd, Earl Shilton, 1995.

*The Airfields of Lincolnshire since 1912,* Ron Blake, Mike Hodgson and Bill Taylor, Midland Counties Publications, Earl Shilton, 1984.

*Airfields of the Eighth, Then and Now*, Roger Freeman, After the Battle, London, 1978.

*Aviation Enthusiasts Guide to London and the South-East*, Peter G Cooksley, Patrick Stephens Ltd, Cambridge, 1986.

*Aviation in Northamptonshire, An Illustrated History*, Michael Gibson, Northamptonshire Libraries, Northampton, 1982.

*Aviation Museums of Britain, Pocket Guide No 2*, Ken Ellis, Midland Publishing, Earl Shilton, 1995.

*British Airfield Buildings of the Second World War, Pocket Guide No 1*, Graham Buchan Innes, Midland Publishing, Earl Shilton, 1995.

*Britain's Aviation Memorials and Mementoes*, David J Smith, Patrick Stephens, Sparkford, 1992.

*British Military Aircraft Serials 1878-1987*, 6th Edition, Bruce Robertson, Midland Counties Publications, Earl Shilton, 1987.

*The Debt We Owe*, Edward Bishop, Longmans, London.

*The Mighty Eighth*, Roger A Freeman, Arms & Armour Press, London, 1986.

*The Squadrons of the Royal Air Force and Commonwealth, 1918-1988*, James J Halley, Air-Britain, Tonbridge, 1988.

*UK Airfields of the Ninth, Then and Now*, Roger Freeman, After the Battle, London, 1990.

*Wrecks & Relics*, 14th Edition, Ken Ellis, Midland Publishing, Earl Shilton, 1994.

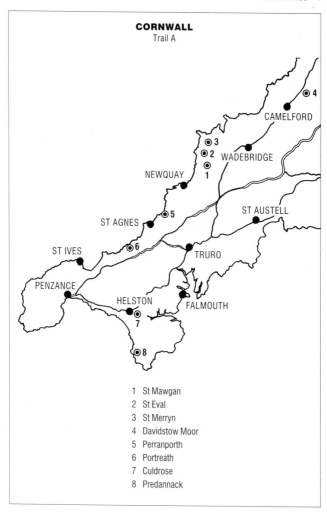

# CORNWALL
## Trail A

1 St Mawgan
2 St Eval
3 St Merryn
4 Davidstow Moor
5 Perranporth
6 Portreath
7 Culdrose
8 Predannack

Without a doubt, Cornwall is a premier holiday county. It entices visitors with golden beaches, excellent resorts and history. The county oozes history, with tales of ship wrecks, smugglers and brave lifeboatmen. The quaint villages, belonging to another age, lead your imagination to the very door of discovery. And so it is with aviation heritage, the airfields act like 'trolley acks' to charge the mind with tangible links to the airmen leaving for the long haul to the Middle East, or an offensive sweep over the Bay of Biscay. Cornwall played its part in closing the dangerous Atlantic gap during the battle against the U-boats, whose menace also had to be subdued during the Normandy expedition, when the threat to the invasion fleet was at its highest. It was from this area that two German submarines were attacked and sunk within 20 minutes by the same crew on the same sortie.

All of this can be felt in Cornwall in a very emotive way, the more so because there are people here who work toward that aim. Those who have contributed toward the upkeep of St Eval church have given us a treasure. There are aviation artists who use their local knowledge to good effect and whose passion for aviation spills into their work. Eddie Simpson makes sure the walls of his pub, the Riviera Inn, are full of aviation prints and he has strong links with the guys at St Mawgan – a marvellous place to recharge the batteries!

**Note**

On the assumption that this trail will be followed while on holiday in Cornwall, times and distances have been taken **from Newquay in each case**, so the trail may be followed in sections throughout your stay.

## ST MAWGAN
5 miles, 10 minutes

*The main gate is signposted off the A3059 Newquay to St Columb Major road.*

RAF St Mawgan is an active airfield and the home of 22 Squadron (with detachments at Chivenor, Devon, Wattisham, Suffolk, and Valley, Anglesey) and the Sea King Training Unit, both operating Westland Sea King HAR.3/3As. (SKTU may take up the 'banner' of 205 Squadron in 1996.) The station is 'guarded' by an Avro Shackleton AEW.2 WL795, although it is well inside the camp and photography is only really possible with prior permission.

Within the Treloy Tourist Park, off the A3059, which occupies one of the domestic sites, can be seen well maintained wartime buildings and the bases of others. From here there are two choices in travelling to the airport side. The shortest route is by way of the A3059 towards St Columb Major, then following signs to the Airport. The longer route is to retrace the A3059 towards Newquay and turn right on to the B3276 to Watergate Bay. This longer route takes in the fire dump (occupied by Shackleton AEW.2 WL756 at the time of writing) and a good vantage point for the runway and airfield layout. Continue to Tregurrian and follow signs to the Airport.

St Mawgan doubles as Newquay Airport, its terminal building being located on the northern side, with access off the B3276. There is a spectator facility on the 'civil side' and it offers good views of the whole airfield. The airport apron utilises wartime 'spectacle' dispersals.

From the airport entrance, face away from the airfield and on the skyline is St Eval airfield, marked by the aerials of the present occupants and the tower of St Eval church.

Wartime buildings survive outside of the present-day boundary of St Mawgan. Paul Shaw

## ST EVAL
4 miles, 10 minutes

*Out of Newquay Airport, turn left, then take the B3276 to Mawgan Porth (and signed Padstow).*

At the top of the descent into Mawgan Porth, is the 'Riviera Inn' on the right. While Eddie and Penny Simpson run this inn, this is a place not to be missed. The walls of every room are full of aviation prints.

Continue down the hill, across the narrow bridge and up the steep rise. On the left hand bend is a sign for St Eval. Turn right and on past the golf course. Take the first left turn, signed St Eval, 1 mile and Padstow 7 miles. In only a few yards, this road swings right onto the line of a runway. The road then uses the perimeter track and along here there are many dispersals to be seen. The second runway is clearly seen but also extends behind the earthen embankment on the outside of the curve. The third runway is found beyond the church and both sides of the road.

No longer used as an airfield, the site is now a communications and signals unit, as witness the many aerials across the airfield. It is however, possible to drive right around the airfield on public roads and gain a good view of what was a classic Coastal Command station. It was from St Eval on 8th June 1944 that a Consolidated Liberator of 224 Squadron achieved the momentous double 'kill' of two U-boats in the space of 22 minutes, in the same sortie.

To build St Eval in 1938, much of the hamlet from which the airfield took its name needed to be knocked down. The church was spared and kept in use as a place of worship for the station personnel. St Eval church is a treasure, not only as a place of prayer, but as a place that reflects upon people who care. Here can be found the last ensign flown from the station, a stained glass window, book of remembrance, wall plaques of squadrons that served from the airfield. The knitted hassocks bear the badges of RAF St Eval and of Coastal Command. If the church is locked, it will be because they have had more vandalism. If it is open, it reflects on their faith and the need to remember.

Looking down St Eval's north west-south east runway, from the perimeter track that now forms the road from Trenance to St Eval. The airfield is littered with transmitter masts. Paul Shaw

A view from almost the same direction of the north west-south east runway, but this time aloft in a model aircraft with remotely operated camera. The public road, using the old perimeter, turns at right angles and heads off towards the church which can just be discerned underneath the wingtip. The extent, and variety, of dispersals is evident. Rod Walker

## ST MERRYN

2 miles, 6 minutes

*Turn left out of St Eval church gate and pass straight through Penrose. At the T junction, give way and turn right and right again.*

St Merryn has plenty to see and do concerning the air. There is a well established gyrocopter club that operates at weekends and a parachute school where all are welcome. The runways are extant but impossible to see from the road. Two hangars survive and can be easily seen as indeed the small control tower can, albeit further away. The largest area of buildings are around the old cinema and are close to the Seagull Tourist Park.

The 'Cornish Arms' public house is on the St Merryn to Padstow road and was the first ward room of HMS *Vulture*, (RNAS St Merryn). A board within the pub commemorates this and the landlord keeps a visitors book of former HMS *Vulture* personnel.

## DAVIDSTOW MOOR

22 miles, 50 minutes

*Use the A389 from Padstow to Wadebridge and follow the A39 north through Camelford. When two transmitter masts can be seen on the skyline, take the right turn signed for Crowdy Reservoir.*

For the most part, the airfield – it was the highest operational airfield in Britain at 970ft above mean sea level – is on agricultural common private land and the cattle grid marks the edge of the airfield. At the cross-

St Merryn retains much of the feel of its RNAS days. Hangars are the Mainhill 'S' type. Paul Shaw

roads following the cattle grid, the right turn to Crowdy Reservoir follows the perimeter track and from this can be seen dispersals and runways. Straight ahead from the cross-roads is the bulk of the airfield with control tower, runways, taxi-tracks, perimeter track and many dispersals. Turning left at the crossroads, the road cuts straight across the main runway and towards the few remaining buildings.

Davidstow Moor has a special quality that makes a visit worthwhile. Despite the years and the state of the control tower, there is not an air of dereliction here. Concrete is in good condition and it is rare to be able to have such easy access to the middle of an airfield which still has complete runways.

## PERRANPORTH
9 miles, 20 minutes

*Take the A3075 and then the B3285 to Perranporth. Stay on the B3285, signed St Agnes, the airfield is on the right.*

At the top of the hill, just before the St George Country Hotel, turn right at the sign board for the Cornish Gliding (and flying) Club, who offer trial lessons. Follow the road and on the left are two large gates on the end of the operational runway 19. Continue along this track to an area suitable to park. The South-west Coast Path is very close and should be followed to the south (left). This path brings a good view of the airfield, the distant control

**The view from the tower at Davidstow Moor.** Paul Shaw

The tower at Davidstow Moor, in skeletal, but sound, condition. Paul Shaw

tower and runways. It also brushes by some of the dispersals, complete with the taxi tracks to them, the revetments and the blast shelters enclosed within the earthen works, all in good condition.

Perranporth airfield retains all three runways and the whole of its perimeter track. This is a busy airfield used by light aircraft and gliders and to that purpose, the control tower is in excellent condition. A hangar to the north of the airfield is extant, and there are a number of dispersals complete with earthen revetments containing blast shelters. These stand on the cliff edge and it is not hard to imagine the miserable winter conditions that servicemen would have had to endure.

There are delights though. To the south on the coastal path is Trevaunance Cove which is the very essence of Cornwall. Beautiful rugged coastline, sandy beach, rock pools and a disused tin mine for a backdrop. The coastal path from the airfield into the cove is very steep and may not be suitable for the elderly or young children. It is possible to reach the cove by car from St Agnes and once there, visitors may be lucky enough to enjoy the sudden impact of sight and sound, of an aircraft taking off from Perranporth, which suddenly appear over the cliff top.

## PORTREATH
9 miles, 24 minutes

*Leave Perranporth airfield by continuing toward St Agnes on the B3285. Leave St Agnes on the B3277 (signed Truro), but turn right at the sign for Porthtowan. Having passed through Porthtowan toward Portreath, at the top of the hill, turn right into Forthvean Road for a view of the airfield.*

Porthreath aerodrome is still in use by the RAF as a communications site and is home to 405 Signals Unit. The airfield does not have a vantage point from which it can be seen and, of course, is off limits. The former WAAF accommodation site, just before the village of Bridge on the B3300 towards Portreath, is in use as factory shops and there are a number of buildings on this site, all in good condition. From the centre of Portreath, the coastal path follows the airfield boundary but yet again, there are only poor views.

Another outlying site is now home to a holiday village and has a public house on site called the 'Ops Room'. To find this, follow the sign for Hayle which goes up the hill from Portreath on the B3301. On the right hand bend at the top, take the left turn for Pool, 3 miles. An attractive pub sign of a Spitfire stands a little way up this road at the top of the drive to the holiday village.

## CULDROSE
16 miles, 25 minutes

*Follow the B3300 from Portreath to
Redruth where signs for A393 Falmouth
should be followed for a short time until
the right turn onto the B3297 signposted
to Helston is seen. When in Helston,
follow signs for A3083, Lizard.*

RNAS Culdrose, otherwise known as HMS
*Seahawk*, is the Navy's biggest shore establishment and the largest military helicopter
base in Europe. The base has three main
roles. Search and rescue for the South West
region by 771 Squadron using red and grey
Westland Sea King HAR.5s. The base is also
parent station to 810, 814 and 820 Squadrons, carrier-borne anti-submarine warfare
units with Sea King HAS.6s and it is also parent to 849 Squadron, the carrier-borne for
airborne early warning unit with Sea King

AEW.2s. Finally, the base is used to train aircrew and other aviation specialists with the
Scottish Aviation Jetstream T.2s of 750
Squadron training observers in airborne navigation, radar handling, low level flying and
continental flight planning. The Westland
Gazelle HT.2 helicopters of 705 Squadron
are prominent in the circuit and are used as a
stepping stone for the student pilots who
then graduate onto the Sea King helicopter.
(The helicopter training role is to be priva-
tised in a new tri-service school at Shaw-
bury, Shropshire.) Also here are the British
Aerospace Hawk T.1s and T.1As of the Fleet
Requirements and Direction Unit, a contractor run target facilities operation. Other
trades taught here are aircrewmen, meteo-
roligists, aircraft handlers and aircraft techni-
cians.

HMS *Seahawk* sits astride the A3083 and
its Hawker Sea Hawk F.1 WF225 gate
guardian can be easily seen on passing, but

**Culdrose 'chopper' of another era, Westland Dragonfly HR.5 at the Cornwall Aero Park.** Daniel Ford

**Westland Sea King AEW.3 of 849 Squadron, Culdrose.** Alan Curry

**Westland Gazelle HT.2 of 705 Squadron, Culdrose.** Ken Ellis

parking is not possible close to. RNAS Culdrose has an excellent spectator area which has the best view of the airfield along with a cafe, shop and toilets. This is an extremely busy airfield and the hangars on the far side can easily be seen. The spectator area is well signposted.

## Cornwall Aero Park

On the northern perimeter of Culdrose, is the Cornwall Aero Park, within the Flambards Village Victorian Theme Park. It is signed off the A3083. Here is a collection of predominantly naval aircraft, and the park offers good views of the activity at Culdrose. There are a wide variety of other attractions here and a cafeteria and shop. (More details on 01326 564093, tourist information centre on site, 01326 565431.)

**Diversion:** In Porthleven, where Guy Gibson grew up, a memorial to his memory was unveiled at the local cemetery on the 19th September 1989 on a plot bought by his cousin, to commemorate the 45th anniversary of his death. (On the B3304 out of Helston, four miles round trip.)

## PREDANNACK
7 miles, 16 minutes

*Follow the A3083 toward Lizard. Having past through Penhale, look out for a derelict wartime building and the airfield is on the right.*

RNAS Predannack is a satellite helicopter training ground to RNAS Culdrose. It has one runway in service condition for fixed wing aircraft and it has landing points for rotary wing aircraft. The Royal Navy Fire School also has a facility here and many airframes are in use for training. A few wartime buildings remain outside the aerodrome site and these are mostly in poor condition. There is a distant but reasonable view of the instructional airframes used by the fire school on the far side of the airfield nearer the coast. Retrace the route and turn left onto the B3296 to Mullion. Pass through Mullion and follow signs for Mullion Cove. A left turn to Predannack should be taken and this road ends at a car park within farm buildings. Footpaths from here will afford views of the airfield.

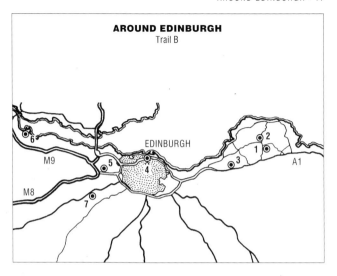

# AROUND EDINBURGH
## Trail B

1 East Fortune
2 Drem
3 Macmerry
4 Edinburgh Castle
5 Turnhouse
6 Grangemouth
7 Kirknewton

It befalls some to have an idea of such simplicity, that they may not even think anything of what they have done. At the Museum of Flight, East Fortune, there are many buildings extant on the technical site. They are brought alive by a notice on each one which states the type of building, the construction and its use. This idea is so very, very effective and, to my knowledge, innovative. Even if one is a keen type on airfield buildings, the setting at East Fortune gives a visual perspective on layout. The dope store is identified along with the forethought to keep other buildings away and to place a fire hydrant nearby. The building with very tall doors? Enjoy the challenge and then step up to the notice to find it is a store for aircraft wings. I enjoyed all of this enormously.

Edinburgh Castle rightly deserves the description of being magnificent! It was yet another gem that offered a unique association with aviation and an opportunity to reflect on the past deeds of the UK's warriors. The 'Shrine', although completely different in looks and feel from the American cemetery at Madingley, Cambridgeshire, captured the same mood of reverence. For those of us who have not seen battle, such venues rightly place a responsibility on us to remember those who have.

Edinburgh is the first city in the British Isles I have visited which did not feel like a city. It felt comfortable, clean, welcoming and without menace. Throughout the tour Edinburgh's Tourist Information Centre (0131 5571700) will prove a fount of information. Those fabulous views of the Firth of Forth were a constant backdrop throughout the trail.

## EAST FORTUNE

*Well signed off the A1 at either East Linton (B1377) or near Haddington (B1347). The entrance to the museum is on the B1347 Haddington road.*

Home of the Museum of Flight. Extensive remains of dispersed domestic sites which are now in industrial use can be found on the lane signposted to Gilmerton.

Just to the north of the museum entrance, the main north east-south west runway crosses the B1347. Here is access to the Sunday market which uses the runway and would give a closer look at the semi-derelict control tower. Access is not possible at other times.

East Fortune has all the runways and perimeter track remaining with four Calendar Hamilton hangars and many buildings extant on the technical site. The majority of these are 'listed' and have notices describing their use, construction and reason for location.

The airfield was brought into commission in 1916, gaining fame as an airship station. There is a memorial marking the first east to west crossing of the Atlantic, and the first double crossing, by the airship R34 which departed from East Fortune on 2nd July 1919. The airfield was used as a satellite of Drem from mid-1940, mostly as a night fighter operational training station.

The museum seeks to chart all aspects of the history of flight in general, while seeking a Scottish 'flavour' whenever possible. The array of exhibits gathered is therefore very wide and includes light aircraft including gliders and hang gliders and rocketry and space flight. There is an impressive air traffic control exhibit. (More details on 01620 880308.)

Memorial marking East Fortune as the departure point for the airship R-34's historic voyage of 1919. Paul Shaw

A view of one of the display hangars at East Fortune. In the foreground is the W-2 autogyro built by G & J Weir at Cathcart, Glasgow, in 1935. Roy Bonser

**Westland Whirlwind I of 263 Squadron in a log blast pen at Drem, July 1940.** J Munro via Dave Smith

**Part of the site at Drem is now used by a haulage contractor.** Paul Shaw

## DREM
3 miles, 9 minutes

*From the main entrance of the Museum of Flight turn right, signed B1347 to North Berwick. Immediately under the railway bridge turn left on the B1377 for Drem. In Drem turn north on the B1345 signed to Dirleton.*

Another airfield built during the First World War with a varied usage but in both wars employed very much in the defence of the Scottish capital. Located to the west of the B1345, the domestic site being closer to Dirleton. Three Bellman hangars are extant, two in good condition. The perimeter track survives, but views of it are hard to come by. Many buildings are in good condition on the domestic site. An overview of the airfield can be seen en route to Macmerry.

## MACMERRY
8 miles, 18 minutes

*Retrace the route to Drem village and take the B1377 to Longniddry. Just after joining the A198, turn left under the railway bridge to the B6363 signed for Pencaitland. Continue over the A1 to Penston.*

The flat area that was Macmerry airfield can easily be distinguished from north of the A1. At Penston there are extensive remains of the domestic site and a beautiful view of the Firth of Forth. The industrial estate south of the junction of the A199 and A1 has some airfield features. Macmerry has also been called Penston airfield, largely because it 'swallowed' the 1914-18 flying site at Penston when the airfield was substantially enlarged in 1942. Macmerry has an interesting history, in that it was developed for civilian flying from 1929 was taken over my the military in 1941 but handed back to Edinburgh Flying Club in 1946, closing finally in 1953.

## EDINBURGH
14 miles, 30 minutes

*Retrace steps to the A1 and follow the signs for Edinburgh city centre and the tourist signs for the castle. A variety of car parks are available.*

Edinburgh Castle has two very interesting aspects of aviation heritage. One is the stained glass memorial window within the Scottish National War Memorial. This is devoted to the Scottish men and women who lost their lives serving with the RFC, RNAS and RAF during both World Wars and conflicts since that time. Within the medallions of the window are aeroplanes, seaplanes, airships and barrage balloons. To either side of the window are groups of flags carved in stone and below, books containing the rolls of honour.

Aviators are also remembered in the Hall of Honour by their inclusion in the rolls of honour of their parent regiment while attached to the RFC. On the outer south wall of the War Memorial is the badge of the RAF below a figure with sword and shield representing courage.

In Crown Square is the Scottish United Services Museum and within are displays of the three services. The RAF display included in 1995 historical accounts of 602 (City of

**Stained glass memorial window in Edinburgh Castle.** Paul Shaw

**Part of the display within the Scottish United Services Museum.** Paul Shaw

Glasgow) and 603 (City of Edinburgh) Squadrons, Royal Auxiliary Air Force, paintings of prominent Scotsmen who served in the RAF and a feature on the WAAF. Displays are changed annually.

A display of the medals of Flight Sergeant George Thompson vc was also to be found, but separate from the remainder of the aviation matter. The son of a Kinross farmer, Thompson was a wireless operator on the Lancasters of 9 Squadron, flying out of Bardney in Lincolnshire. On New Year's Day 1945 9 Squadron took part in a daylight raid on the Dortmund-Ems canal. After the bombs had gone, the 'Lanc' – piloted by New Zealander Flying Officer F H Denton – took a series of hits, shattering the nose and causing a series of fires in the fuselage. Thompson rescued both the mid upper and rear gunners from their blazing positions, extinguishing fires on

their clothing with his bare hands. Denton executed a good crash-landing in the Netherlands. One of the gunners died, but the other survived. Thompson died in hospital from pneumonia brought about partly by his horrific burns and frost bite experienced in the shattered fuselage. (More details on Edinburgh Castle on 0131 2204733.)

## TURNHOUSE
7 miles, 28 minutes

*From the castle, follow the signs for Glasgow A8 and Edinburgh Airport. When close to the boundary of Edinburgh Airport a road on the right goes to the main gate.*

RAF Turnhouse closed on 1st April 1996. The airfield opened in 1916 and was the home of 603 (City of Edinburgh) Squadron, Royal Auxiliary Air Force from its formation in 1925 through to disbandment in March 1957 (other than wartime operational deployments). The airfield became Edinburgh Airport in 1947, with a terminal building opening in 1956. In the early 1970s a brand new runway (07/23) was built to cope with the expansion of traffic and a new terminal building, all to the west of the original airfield. There are spectator facilities on the 'new' airport site.

As this was written, the fate of the RAF side of the airport had not been decided. Many buildings, most of the 'Expansion Period' type are extant and in excellent condition. A full-scale replica Spitfire in the colours of 603 Squadron is displayed on a plinth outside the former station headquarters, ben-

eath it a plaque in memory of those members of the unit who gave their lives in the service of their country. It is not known if the Spitfire replica and the memorial will remain on this site, or be relocated.

## GRANGEMOUTH
20 miles, 30 minutes

*DIVERSION: Retrace the route to the A8 and follow signs for Glasgow M8 and Stirling M9. Join the M9 and leave at Junction 5 and follow signs for the industrial estate.*

Grangemouth is an airfield that has ceased to exist to all intents and purposes, but there are clues to its presence. To the north and east

**KLM Dutch Airlines Douglas DC-2 PH-ASR outside the terminal building at Grangemouth during the official opening ceremony on 1st May 1939.** via J Walker

lies the huge oil refinery and complex. Also to the east is the River Avon, taking a sharp right bend and forming what was the airfields eastern boundary. To the west lies Zetland Park. Bo'Ness Road marks the northern boundary and here can be found a small cairn erected in 1993 to mark the site of the airfield. Within the Abbotsinch Industrial Estate are two large warehouses, closer inspection reveals these to have been two of the original hangars, from the airfield's opening on 1st May 1939 as Central Scotland Airport. At least one building still has the winged lion badge of Scottish Aviation, who used to operate the airport. Backtrack down Bo'Ness Road from the hangars to the roundabout at Inchyra Road, turn down here (signed Inchyra Industrial Estate and Sports Stadium). This odd-looking 'dual carriageway' follows exactly the north east-south west runway.

Retrace steps back to Junction 5 of the M9 and go eastbound to its end, then take the A8 towards Edinburgh and past Edinburgh Airport. At the junction with the A720 turn left and rejoin he trail.

## KIRKNEWTON
13 miles, 21 minutes

*From the former RAF Turnhouse, rejoin the A8 and travel towards the Edinburgh city by-pass. Turn left at the junction with the A720 and follow this until the junction with the A70, take this (signed Currie). Continue down the A70 to the junction with the B7031, signed Kirknewton.*

Home of 661 Volunteer Gliding School, flying Grob Vikings, Kirknewton is also occupied by the army and the Ministry of Defence. Runways and perimeter track survive, but are in decaying state. There are three hangars and some buildings on the military side, the hangars are clad in asbestos sheet and one has had the doors welded up, functioning as a drill hall. The domestic site stands well back on the opposite side of the B7031 and is a mixture of wartime and post-war buildings, all of which were due for demolition in 1996.

**To return to East Fortune**: Retrace the route along the B7031 and the A70 to the Edinburgh ring road (A720). Follow signs for Berwick upon Tweed and A1. The Museum of Flight at East Fortune is well signposted off the A1 east of Haddington. (34 miles, 50 minutes.)

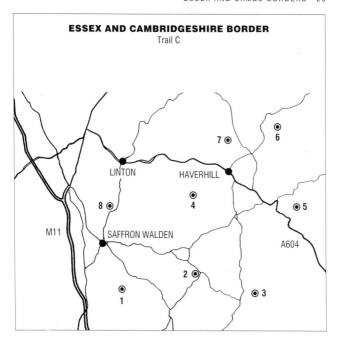

**ESSEX AND CAMBRIDGESHIRE BORDER**
Trail C

1 Debden
2 Great Sampford
3 Wethersfield
4 Castle Camps
5 Ridgewell
6 Stradishall
7 Wratting Common
8 Little Walden

I have always held preconceived ideas about Essex. Following my visit to this area, I have had to change them. There are more thatched roofs per square mile on buildings that have a distinctive style. The layout and siting of these buildings is also unique, giving a very individual flavour. Saffron Walden is a place I must return to. I was not aware of its charm and had not allowed enough time to wander around. Narrow streets are filled with timber framed houses and shops, including those where the upper floors protrude over the pavement. The local geography meant that the airfields had an infinite feeling of space, seemingly so close to the heavens. The sensation is at odds with the actual height above sea level. Little Walden gave the explorer in me an enjoyable outing. Ridgewell had an aura where I felt the need to rush to the library and find out what had happened there. Regrets? Only that I did not have time to stop at just one of the many idyllic-looking rural public houses that were dotted along the route .

## SAFFRON WALDEN

A lovely little town with narrow streets and many timber framed houses. The Anglo-American Memorial sits in a park on the northern edge of town but within easy walking distance of the shops. The memorial occupies a tranquil place close to where people enjoy their leisure. Football, cricket, children's park, bowls and shopping, all have a gentle reminder to whom such freedoms are owed. Cleverly arranged so one has to step inside this sanctuary, it is bordered by a hedgerow within which is a rose garden. A large stone tablet in the centre of the memorial notes that it is dedicated to the 65th Fighter Wing, USAAF and the men and women of the borough who gave their lives in the defence of freedom 1939-45. On the flanks of this tablet are other stone tablets carrying the names of those who died, headed by the Fighter Group with which they served. These were the 4th (Debden and Steeple Morden), 56th (Halesworth), 355th (Steeple Morden), 361st (Little Walden) and 479th (Wattisham) Fighter Groups. The memorial is near the cricket pavilion which lies behind the Saffron Walden Football Club. A free car park is signposted off the Little Walden road near the 'Victory' public house.

## DEBDEN

4 miles, 8 minutes

*Return to the centre of Saffron Walden, then follow signs for the B184, Thaxted. The road rises from Saffron Walden and the large scanner dish of Debden National Air Traffic Services radar station, identifies the western side of the old airfield.*

Debden airfield is now called Carver Barracks and is the home of 33 Engineer Regiment who handle explosive ordnance disposal. The familiar sights of expansion period architecture can still be seen. An eight bay 'C' type hangar, Officers' mess, married quarters and the guardroom. A machine gun post can be seen behind the houses opposite the main gate. Also opposite the main gate is an enlarged blister hangar. The best view of the airfield from the B184 has been lost through the placement of an earthen embankment. A good view of a runway can be

**The Anglo-American war memorial at Saffron Walden.** Paul Shaw

easily found from the public road along with a blister hangar and pill box. There is a memorial to the 4th Fighter Group USAAF here but it is just inside the main gate.

## GREAT SAMPFORD
3 miles, 10 minutes

*Retrace the route to the B184 and turn right then left for Radwinter, 3 miles. Continue along this road to Wimbish Green. Note the wartime buildings in a yard and residential properties opposite that have made use of wartime structures. Take the right turn for Wimbish Lower Green, a no through road.*

A small concrete road straight ahead forms a public footpath that gives access to the edge of the airfield. Further east, a public footpath goes straight across the old airfield. Great Sampford is an airfield where only the perimeter track remains extant. To compensate, there are many outlying wartime buildings to be found, some used for light industrial work, some still in use as residential properties. The airfield had but a fleeting history, opened in April 1942, with its temporarily resident fighter units flying from Sommerfeld strip runways. It closed in August 1944.

## WETHERSFIELD
8 miles, 18 minutes

*DIVERSION: Join the B1053 at Great Sampford and turn right, signed Wethersfield and Braintree. Once through Finchingfield, minor roads to the right offer limited vantage points.*

This is a huge airfield, with few places that afford a real view. Today it is a reserve airfield, capable of use for exercises, but is mainly the domain of the Ministry of Defence Police, who use it as a training ground. It is self-evident that it is very much operational and out of bounds! It also plays host to the Army Air Corps helicopters from Wattisham and at weekends the Viking T.1 gliders of 614 Volunteer Gliding School can be seen.

Retrace the route on the B1053 to Great Sampford to rejoin the trail.

## CASTLE CAMPS
8 miles, 18 minutes

*Join the B1054 in Radwinter, following the signs for Haverhill. Within three miles take the left turn for Helions Bumpstead and then follow signs for Castle Camps.*

The road to Castle Camps from Helions Bumpstead climbs gradually until the area of the old airfield is reached. Two public footpaths give access across the old airfield from the Camps End to Olmstead Green Road. The area of the old airfield followed the majority on this trail for occupying the high

**Brick memorial at Castle Camps.** Paul Shaw

ground. Little remains, which hardly seems possible for a once busy aerodrome. The perimeter track survives at farm track width. Only two wartime structures could be found, but a welcome addition is the brick memorial on the edge of the airfield unveiled on the 11th September 1994 dedicated to all units who served from the airfield.

## RIDGEWELL
10 miles, 23 minutes

*Retrace the route to Helions Bumpstead and follow signs for Steeple Bumpstead. Join the B1054 and stay on the B1054 until meeting the A604, turn right for Colchester. After passing straight through Ridgewell village, close to Oaker Hill is the memorial on the left.*

A helpful marker for the proximity of the memorial are the two long Nissen-like buildings. Dominated by the 'Triangle L' of the B-17 Flying Fortress equipped 381st Bombardment Group, the memorial is an impressive sight. From the memorial retrace the route north west up the A604 and turn off right to Tilbury Green. The old airfield and surrounding area has a lot to offer, pride of place being the chance to drive around part of the perimeter track that has been reduced to road width. Two runways have been reduced to farm track width and a gliding club use a grass runway for their activities. Part of the station sick quarters survives, along with a domestic site and two large buildings, one of which looked to have been the gymnasium.

The minor road from Ashen to Great Yeldham uses much of the old perimeter track, and to the south of this lay the

**The impressive memorial to the 81st Bombardment Group at Ridgewell.** Paul Shaw

technical site, either side of the road to Tilbury Green. Looking north from the T-junction where the Tilbury Green road joins the perimeter track is the site where the control tower was. In similar manner the present day minor road from Pannel's Ash to Ovington also uses a section of perimeter track, the pronounced bend, marking the threshold of what was the north east-south west runway.

In Ridgewell itself is the 'King's Head' which has photos and newspaper clippings from the airfield's past on display. It was a favourite haunt of American airmen.

## STRADISHALL
11 miles, 19 minutes

*Join the A1092, signed Long Melford. In the centre of Clare, follow Newmarket, B1063. After Stradishall, follow sings for the prison, westbound on the A143.*

Just off route in the village of Hundon is a memorial and a village sign that have aviation connections. RAF Stradishall lay within the parish boundary. Stradishall village also has a commemorative sign. Within Stradishall village, the church of St Margaret's houses a stained glass memorial window, dedicated to the 640 people who gave their lives whilst serving at RAF Stradishall, some of whom are buried in the graveyard. A book of remembrance is also kept in the church.

The station buildings at Stradishall are in very good condition following the recent closure as an active RAF establishment in August 1970. The site is now HM Prison High Point and this curtails any investigations. Do not let this deter anyone from finding the memorial which stands close to Stirling House, the old Officers' Mess. Stirling House is now a Home Office training centre, and a room had been fashioned as an officers' mess. The work is on-going to also house memorabilia and documents, but it is not planned for there to be admittance to the public.

## WRATTING COMMON
10 miles, 18 minutes

*Continue along the A143 toward Haverhill from the prison. Take the right turn on a minor road for Little Thurlow. Pass through Little Thurlow and at the B1061, turn left. In only a few hundred yards, turn right for Carlton Green. At the junction in Carlton Green, turn left for Horseheath and West Wickham.*

It is an oddity of man that something which delights one, leaves the other wondering what all the fuss is about. There is a 'T2' hangar at Wratting Common (or West Wickham as it was originally known) which ought to receive best of breed and best at show awards. There is a small supporting cast of a 'B1' and a modern clad (with roller shutter doors) 'T2', but the lack of an aerodrome feel means Wratting Common will never be the equivalent of a West End musical hit. The granite memorial is on the Carlton Green to West Wickham road against a farm building on the left. This was dedicated on 28th May 1989 in memory of the Short Stirling units that flew from here, 90 and 195 Squadrons and 1651 Heavy Conversion Unit.

## LITTLE WALDEN
11 miles, 20 minutes

*Continue on the road to Horseheath, and join the A1307 (formerly A604) to Cambridge. In Linton, turn left at the sign for Hadstock and Saffron Walden, the B1052. Travel straight through Hadstock and the former airfield is either side of the road.*

There are many ways to enjoy a visit to old airfields. Some airfields are brash and reveal all at once. Some are so perfect, it is a delight just to stand and look. Some have disappeared, yet retain a presence. Some are still a hive of activity. Some are museums with free access. Some are out of bounds. Little Walden had its own special feel. Seemingly obvious at first, further exploration brought rewards. Do not accept Little Walden at face value. It seemed to have a way of revealing a little at time.

The Douglas A-20 Havocs of 409th Bombardment Group first operated from here, followed by the North American P-51 Mustangs of the 361st Fighter Group in the summer of 1944. Flying ceased in November 1945, but the airfield was not disposed of until 1960.

The B1052 cuts straight across the airfield giving good access and uses the former north east-south west runway as its base for the portion that runs past the control tower. The perimeter track has been utilised for access to a haulage and warehousing company, and a farm. A public footpath gives further access across the airfield and two runways of farm track make for comfortable walking. Among sights to be seen are the control tower in excellent condition (used as offices), two 'T2' hangars, enlarged blister hangars, parachute store, fire tender shed and barrack huts.

**To return to Saffron Walden**: Continue on the B1052 for Saffron Walden. The Anglo-American memorial is off this road on the northern edge of the town. (4 miles, 7 minutes.)

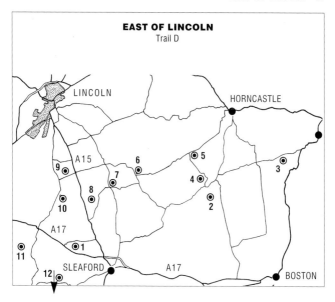

**EAST OF LINCOLN**
Trail D

1  Cranwell
2  Coningsby
3  East Kirkby
4  Thorpe Camp
5  Woodhall Spa
6  Metheringham
7  Scopwick
8  Digby
9  Coleby Grange
10 Wellingore
11 Fulbeck
12 Barkston Heath

It is easy to imagine that the flat countryside on this trail makes everything stand out. Perhaps it does. What does stand out are the memories I have of this area, for there are special places and special moments to be enjoyed. They include two Lancasters that can be seen in motion, Tornadoes on active duty, the handsome memorial at Woodhall Spa, and roads that use the perimeter track and a runway at Metheringham. The Royal Air Force College building is most impressive, but I took as much pleasure in spotting a road opposite the guardroom named after T E Lawrence (of Arabia fame).

I have joined those who are always to be found waiting for Lancaster PA474 to come home, and it released many emotions when she taxied in. Pride, elation, nostalgia, sadness, reflection, wonder and gratitude are but a few. Whatever, there was the sheer joy of watching and listening.

In years to come, there will be those who might reflect on their luck in being privy to Mr Panton's memories. For one felt privileged to have been allowed to share them with him. The airfield tour of East Kirkby gave me such a buzz, I wrote as much down as I could remember, so I might never forget. The spectacle of the engine run ups at East Kirkby are a much more intimate affair than at Coningsby. There is also a chance of a photograph with the control tower in the background.

A welcome addition to the many aviation venues is the Thorpe Camp Visitor Centre. Welcome, because it allows one to gain an insight into the environs of wartime airmen when not on duty.

While geographically within an easy day's drive, this trail should be done over two days to allow time to absorb everything these venues have to offer. The following, however, may influence a decision on timing a visit to this area. The Battle of Britain Memorial Flight (BBMF) hangar is not open to the public at weekends. However, it is often possible to see the aircraft of the Flight depart and arrive at weekends. The Lincolnshire Aviation Heritage Centre is not open on Sundays and is most likely to have its Lancaster do engine run-ups on Saturdays. Thorpe Camp is only open on Sunday afternoons. Coningsby and Cranwell are both very quiet during weekends. So this should give plenty of scope! A three-day 'weekend' could be the answer. Friday to include BBMF, Saturday East Kirkby and Sunday Thorpe Camp.

The area is the home to the mother of all aviation trails, the award-winning Lincolnshire Aviation Heritage Trail (LAHT) pioneered and run by North Kesteven District Council and in part the inspiration for this title. Former airfields have been marked with special signs and there is a superb booklet detailing the points on the trail and the growing number of heritage centres. (More details of the booklet and the trail on 01529 414294.)

## CRANWELL

### On the B1429 north west of Sleaford.

Buildings within the Royal Air Force College, including the magnificent college itself, can be comprehensively viewed from the B1429 which runs through the famous camp. A BAC Jet Provost T.5A is on display. The airfield, with two runways, is easily viewed from the A17 Sleaford to Newark road. Recently, Cranwell has witnessed an influx of aircraft and currently hosts 45(R) Squadron flying Scottish Aviation Jetstream T.1s; the RAF Aerobatic Team, the 'Red Arrows' on British Aerospace Hawk T.1 and T.1As; 3 Flying

**The magnificent facade of the Royal Air Force College at Cranwell.** Ken Ellis

**Ornate gates to the College, carrying the RAF badge and motto *Per Ardua ad Astra*.** Paul Shaw

Training School using Scottish Aviation Bulldog T.1s (pooled with the Central Flying School and JEFTS – see under Barkston Heath below) and Hawker Siddeley Dominie T.1s and T.2s. Additionally, there are the Airframe Technology Flight and Service Instruction Flight both with grounded instructional airframes. The grass airfield to the north of the college buildings is used for gliding and is not readily viewable.

Within Cranwell village is the church of St Andrew. The graveyard contains the graves of many airmen, some of them dating from Cranwell's First World War days when it was a Royal Naval Air Station, HMS *Daedalus*.

Retrace the route from Cranwell village back down the B1429 towards the RAF College, but turn south (left) on the minor road to North and South Rauceby, cross the A17 and on the right is the Cranwell Aviation Heritage Centre, and another Jet Provost 'guardian', this time T.4 XP556. Within the centre (which

is also a Tourist Information Centre) is a superb display on the history of Cranwell and on the other airfields in the LAHT. (Details of opening etc on 01529 488490.)

## CONINGSBY

18 miles, 34 minutes

*Join the A17 and head east, signed Sleaford and Boston. Turn left on to the A153, signed Horncastle and Skegness. The Battle of Britain Memorial Flight Heritage Centre is well signed to the south of the A153 at Coningsby.*

Coningsby is very much in the front-line flying the Panavia Tornado F.3 air defence fighter. Resident are 5 and 29 Squadrons, with 56(R) Squadron acting as the operational conversion unit. Also here is the F.3 Operational Evaluation Unit, part of the Air Warfare Centre.

Views of the Tornado comings and goings are best had by a short walk down from the Battle of Britain Memorial Flight Visitor Centre on the lane to Dogdyke. This is an incredibly noisy area when jets are flying and can be frightening for young children.

The Visitor Centre has its own car park and it is not unusual to catch the Avro Lancaster outside, perhaps with the engine cowlings off, doing run ups. To see flames belching from the Merlin exhausts on start up is magic! Telephone the Visitor Centre on weekdays only on 01526 344041 to see if the aircraft of the BBMF will be in the hangar on the day intended to visit. They will supply estimated arrival and departure times of the aircraft if they are operating.

Each year, the Flight issues a detailed programme of is commitments and these can be used to identify those days when only a short flight is involved and the aircraft will probably depart and return in a short time – this will help to coincide viewing with flight activity. Be warned, these are precious aircraft and they are not operated in adverse weather conditions. This may mean that advice given in good faith can be wrong on the day of travel, if weather has delayed aircraft at another venue.

If already in the area, a notice board just along from the Flight hangar gives dates and times of sorties for the following week. Even if the Flight are away on the airshow circuit, the Visitor Centre is well worth a visit with a wide array of exhibitions and artefacts including a GRAND SLAM and TALLBOY bombs. There is also a well stocked shop.

**The Battle of Britain Memorial Flight Visitor Centre at Coningsby allows visitors close views of the aircraft, when not at airshows. During the winter, fascinating views of maintenance work can be had.** Ken Ellis

## EAST KIRKBY
10 miles, 15 minutes

*Retrace the route on to the A153 and turn right for Horncastle. (Note the unusual clock face on the tower of Coningsby Church.) Turn right on the A155, signed Spilsby. Having passed through East Kirkby village, the centre is on the right and well signed.*

The station was the base for 57 and 630 Squadrons, who flew Lancasters. Just inside the entrance is a memorial to both units. Lancaster VII NX611 is maintained in running order by the Lincolnshire Aviation Heritage Centre (LAHC) and is painted in the colours of 57 Squadron (as 'DX-C' *Just Jane*) on the starboard side and 630 Squadron (as 'LE-C') on the port side. The 'Lanc' is run up and taxied on chosen Saturdays during the summer. (A call on 01790 763207 will provide details of expected 'running' dates, plus details of opening times etc. Note that the LAHC is not open on Sundays.)

The control tower has been restored and the upper room refitted to the point where it is difficult to find a difference between how it is now and a display photograph of how it was during the war. Many other displays, airframes and equipment make this a marvellous venue which will take at least half a day to view properly.

Something not to be missed is the airfield tour on the back of a 'Queen Mary' trailer. Fred Panton will often be the guide and his commentary of his childhood memories of the 'Lancs' arriving and the atmosphere of the time, make this an event to cherish. Mr Panton may also talk of 17th April 1945 when there was an accident with Lancaster III PB360 of 57 Squadron. Two bombs detonated, causing a 'domino' effect. Three airmen perished and 14 were seriously injured, five 'Lancs' written off and 14 damaged.

**Memorial to 57 and 630 Squadrons at the entrance to the Lincolnshire Aviation Heritage Centre at East Kirkby.** Ken Ellis

## TATTERSHALL THORPE
12 miles, 25 minutes

*Retrace the route from East Kirkby to Coningsby and turn right on to the B1192 for Woodhall Spa. Thorpe Camp is on the left beyond the 'Blue Bell Inn'.*

Thorpe Camp Visitor Centre occupies the former No 1 Communal Site of RAF Woodhall Spa. Open on Sundays and Bank Holidays (other times by appointment) it uses the original buildings to show life in wartime Lincolnshire and the history of the airfield and its units. (For more details contact Woodhall Spa tourist information centre on 01526 353775.) Recent acquisitions are two buoys and a section of anti-torpedo netting which was used to protect the warship *Tirpitz*. During its time at Woodhall Spa, 617 Squadron were involved in overcoming such obstacles to sink this ship.

Also worth a visit (although it has restricted opening times) is the 'Blue Bell Inn' within Tattershall Thorpe, which displays many photographs on its walls, most from Woodhall Spa.

**Part of the 617 Squadron display within the Thorpe Camp Visitor Centre.** Ken Ellis

## WOODHALL SPA
3 miles, 5 minutes

*Continue north on the B1192.*

Only a mile north from Thorpe Camp, on the right is Woodhall Spa airfield. The northern edge of the airfield is still in use, as RAF Woodhall, and involved in the ground testing of RB.199 turbojets for Coningsby's Tornados. The approach road to this restricted area uses some of the original perimeter track and here two dispersals can be seen. Much of the rest of the airfield is used for gravel extraction and the access road here is a reduced width piece of runway.

Woodhall Spa itself is a delightful place with a tranquil feel. The striking 'Dambusters' memorial is located prominently at the junction of the B1191 and B1192.

At this junction, heading north is a minor road to Stixwould, travel up this a short distance and on the right is the 'Petwood House Hotel', a very attractive building set in extensive grounds. This was the officer's mess for 617 Squadron during their tenure at Woodhall Spa and the hotel contains much memorabilia. *(More details in Aeronautical Pubs & Inns of Britain.)*

**Diversion**: Woodhall Spa bomb dump. Follow the B1191 towards Horncastle and turn right into Kirkby Lane at the sign for Kirkby on Bain. In a mile turn right on to an unmarked road, a short distance past the cemetery. This leads to Ostler's Plantation which is Forestry Commission land and where the public are welcome. Use the car park and five minutes walk along the stone road produces the sight of concrete roads and derelict buildings, this was the extensive bomb dump. Retrace steps back into Woodhall Spa to rejoin the trail.

A view of the present day RAF Woodhall, in the foreground is wartime perimeter track. Ken Ellis

## METHERINGHAM
6 miles, 12 minutes

*From Woodhall Spa, follow the B1191 to Martin just before the junction with the B1189, turn right, signposted Blankney Fen and Blankney Barff Walks. The Memorial Room is well signposted.*

Metheringham airfield retains the look of an airfield and offers a rare opportunity to travel along its perimeter track and one of its runways. While the other two runways have been removed, one cannot mistake where they were. Wartime buildings remain in reasonable condition and are used by industry. The control tower is in ruins but the airfield does have an excellent Memorial Room on a former dispersed site. This charts the history of the airfield from opening to closure on boards on the walls. (More details on 01526 378270 or from Sleaford tourist information on 01529 414249.) There is an impressive brick memorial to 106 Squadron who flew Lancasters from here November 1943 to February 1946.

## SCOPWICK
5 miles, 12 minutes

*Take the B1189 toward Billinghay. Turn right on to the B1191 signposted to Scopwick. Continue through Scopwick to the junction with the B1188. Turn right and at the next crossroads in only a few hundred yards, turn right into Vicarage Lane.*

The village burial ground is the last resting place of many airmen, predominantly Canadians because of the strong link with Digby.

## DIGBY
2 miles, 3 minutes

*Take the road opposite Vicarage Lane, signposted for RAF Digby.*

Digby is still an operational base, being the home of 399 Signals Unit and the Aerial Erector's School. The airfield is now an aerial

Updated 'Expansion Period' buildings within RAF Digby. Ken Ellis

farm and no flying takes place here. Views of the buildings are possible from public roads, most from the 'Expansion Period'. A full scale replica Spitfire, in the colours of 416 (RCAF) Squadron is mounted on a pole and memorials to those who served on the station from 1918 and to 411 (RCAF) Squadron can be found within the base, but viewable only by prior permission.

## COLEBY GRANGE
6 miles, 12 minutes

*From Digby head west for the A15 (probably via Ashby de la Launde) and turn right on to it, signed for Lincoln. After the crossing of the B1202 the airfield is immediately on the left.*

A grass aerodrome with a concrete perimeter track, initially established as a relief landing ground for Cranwell in 1940. It became an active fighter base and is mainly associated with Bristol Beaufighters. From 1959 to 1963 the airfield was used to house Thor ballistic

missiles of 142 Squadron and their hard standings can confuse those trying to define the Second World War layout. East of the A!5 is Heath House and here is evidence of wartime concrete, indeed a hangar stood here, the cafe on the west side showing signs of concrete that probably formed the taxi track to connect the airfield with the dispersed site. Views of the skeletal control tower can be had from the A15 and from the B1202. The perimeter track extended over the B1202 and there are places where this is easily defined.

## WELLINGORE
5 miles, 8 minutes

*Continue westwards on the B1202, then turn left on to the A607, signed Grantham.*

In Navenby, on the left, can be found the 'Lion and Royal' public house. This is famous as the billet Guy Gibson used when he was stationed at Wellingore and is referred to in his book, *Enemy Coast Ahead*.

The actual room has been lost in alterations past, but there is plenty of interest here and the pub does offer accommodation. (See the companion volume *Aeronautical Pubs & Inns of Britain* for more details.)

Across the road from the 'Lion and Royal' is the Navenby Heritage Room, which includes displays on the local RAF stations as well as local history. (Further information from Sleaford tourist information on 01529 414249). In the Old Station, the Flight Simulation Centre has been established offering 'flights' in a series of full-axis former RAF simulators. (Contact 01522 810388.)

Leave Navenby and continue south on the A607 for a short distance and take the left fork signposted Wellingore Picnic Site. Stay on this road and at Heath Farm a pillbox denotes the perimeter of the former RAF Wellingore. This was another relief landing ground, with metalled perimeter and grass airfield and occupied intermittently by fighter units. The eastern boundary was the Roman road Ermine Street. Apart from some pillboxes, some earthen blast pens can be discerned.

## FULBECK
10 miles, 18 minutes

*DIVERSION: Rejoin the A607 and head into Leadenham. Turn right on the A17, signed Newark. Turn left on the minor road signed Stragglethorpe and Marston.*

Last used in 1970 as a relief landing ground for Cranwell, much remains on the site. To return to the trail, retrace steps to the A17 and head east towards Sleaford from Cranwell.

## BARKSTON HEATH
15 miles, 25 minutes

*DIVERSION: From Wellingore, continue south on the minor road, then turn left on the A17 signed Sleaford. Turn right on to the B6403, signed Ancaster and Colsterworth. The airfield is south of the A153 crossroads.*

Home of the civilian-run Joint Elementary Flying Training School flying Slingsby T.67 Fireflies, Barkston Heath is an operational RAF airfield and therefore out of bounds. Good views can be had of the flying from the B6403, Willoughby Heath and the minor road to Barkston. To the east of the B6403 is a hangar complex, now used for industry. To rejoin the trail retrace steps to the A17, then turn right for Cranwell.

**To return to Cranwell:** Continue south on the minor road, then turn left on the A17 signed Sleaford and pick up the signs for Cranwell.

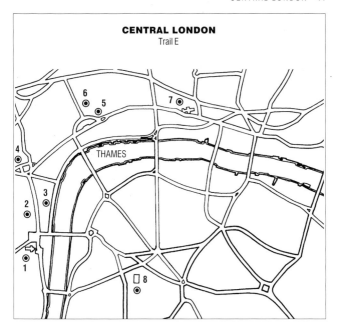

# CENTRAL LONDON
Trail E

1 Westminster Abbey
2 Whitehall
3 Embankment
4 Trafalgar Square
5 St Clement Dane's
6 Kingsway
7 St Paul's Cathedral
8 Imperial War Museum

London for me will forever be the sound of four Merlin engines echoing off the buildings around the church of St Clement Dane's when the Battle of Britain Memorial Flight Lancaster came along Fleet Street to execute a precision timed flypast, as the bugler finished the 'Last Post'. Then followed the unveiling of the statue of Sir Arthur T Harris.

In keeping with the prestige of the capital, London has many tangible links with our aviation heritage. There are too many for anyone to single out a favourite, but there are some very special monuments to be enjoyed.

Unlike the other trails, the best way to progress on this one is by foot and recommendations are made at venues where suitable public transport is available to those that are only a little way out. London Transport Travel Information Centres are plentiful and there is a central number for information on 0171 2221234. Make use also of the good services of the London Tourist Board on 0171 7303450.

## WESTMINSTER ABBEY

Throughout the British Isles and indeed the world, memorials will frequently mention valour in the cause of freedom. It seems appropriate to begin in Parliament Square, against the Mother of All Parliaments. Here is Westminster Abbey and within the eastern most apse of Henry VII's Chapel is the Royal Air Force Chapel. Here a memorial window is dedicated to pilots who lost their lives during the Battle of Britain. The window, dedicated on 10th July 1947, was designed by Hugh Easton and comprises four panels depicting airmen. Between the Royal Arms and the badge of the RAF are the flags of Australia, Belgium, Canada, Czechoslovakia, New Zealand, Poland, South Africa and the USA. The branches of a rose tree entwine the badges of those units that took part in the battle. A roll of honour to those killed in the battle is nearby and the chapel is the burial place of Lord Dowding and Lord Trenchard. A special opening on Wednesday evenings is the only time that photography is allowed within the Abbey. There is no viewing on Sundays. More specific information on 0171 222 5152.

Close by, on Horse Guards' Parade are the Cabinet War Rooms, below the Treasury. Preserved exactly as they were in wartime, there are 21 rooms, including the Cabinet Room, Map Room and Churchill's bedroom. (More details on 0171 9306961.)

**Diversion:** Here is an option to head west for the Science Museum. Best method is to use Westminster Underground and the Circle & District Lines to South Kensington.

## WHITEHALL

Leave Parliament Square by way of Parliament Street. Pass by the Cenotaph, before moving on to the Ministry of Defence, on the right, in Whitehall - note the badges of the RAF that flank the entrance. Retrace the route and turn left into Richmond Terrace, opposite Downing Street. Turn left into Victoria Embankment. The statues of Lord Trenchard and Viscount Portal of Hungerford are in the gardens, with the Ministry of Defence behind them.

## THE EMBANKMENT

Further along the Embankment is the RAF Memorial. Having turned against the idea of a tri-service memorial opposite Buckingham Palace, the RAF Memorial Fund committee hoped to site the memorial between St Margaret's church and Westminster Abbey, but were unsuccessful. The memorial is of Portland stone and surmounted by a gilded eagle sculpted by W Reid Dick. The eagle symbolically faces towards France, across the river. It was unveiled by HRH The Prince of Wales (Edward VIII to be) on 16th July 1923.

## TRAFALGAR SQUARE

Continue along the Embankment to Northumberland Avenue, which leads directly to Trafalgar Square. In the far right, northern, corner is the church of St Martin in the Fields opposite the National Gallery. Within the church is a bust commemorating the Glider Pilot Regiment and dedicated on 25th July 1958.

**Diversion:** This is a good point in the tour to head south west to the Science Museum. Buses run from Trafalgar Square along the Kensington Road. The Science Museum is behind the Albert Hall, reached down Exhibition Road. Or take the Charing Cross underground one stop southbound on the Northern Line and then westbound on the Circle & District to South Kensington.

## ST CLEMENT DANE'S

Buses run from Trafalgar Square to St Clement Dane's, the Strand and Aldwych. Or use the Charing Cross underground Northern Line one stop southbound, then the Circle & District eastbound to Temple.

St Clement Dane's is the Royal Air Force church. A victim of the 'blitz', it was chosen by the RAF for a number of complementary reasons, to restore it from the ruin it had become. There are statues outside the church of Lord Dowding, Commander-in-Chief of Fighter Command during the Battle of Britain and Sir Arthur Harris, Commander-in-Chief of Bomber Command during the Second World War. Lord Tedder's ashes are buried in the church and there are books of remembrance with 19,000 American and 125,000 British, Commonwealth and other Allied countries inside. There are 735 floor tiles carrying the squadron and unit badges of the RAF. While walking around the church, deep marks can be seen in the walls. These are the result of bomb splinters and have been deliberately left in place. The church is open for public viewing daily, more details on 0171 7303450.

## KINGSWAY

In The Strand, the 'Hotel Cecil' was used by the Royal Naval Air Service during the Great War and by the Air Board in 1917. The Air Board was succeeded by the Air Ministry and Hugh Trenchard became the first Chief of Air Staff, using the 'Cecil' as its base. The Air Staff moved to 'Adastral House' in 1919.

Returned from a ruin, the RAF church of St Clement Dane's in The Strand. Paul Shaw

Walk into the Aldwych and turn right into Kingsway, a bronze plaque marks the place that was 'Adastral House' 1919-55. The Strand must have seen every one of the RAF's top men, some of whom are remembered in St Clement Dane's.

## ST PAUL'S CATHEDRAL

The walk along the Strand, into Fleet Street and Ludgate Hull to the Cathedral is full of interest. There are buses for those who wish!

Within the Cathedral is the American Memorial Chapel which contains a roll of honour for those 28,000 Americans who lost their lives on operations from Britain during the Second World War. There is a book of remembrance for the Air Transport Auxiliary pilots who lost their lives while ferrying aircraft and a memorial erected by the RAF Escaping Society to those who helped Allied airmen to escape or evade captivity.

The Cathedral is open to public viewing Monday to Saturday, Sunday is for worship only. To view the aviation-related elements, a ticket for the Cathedral floor and crypt will suffice. More details on 0171 2482705.

## IMPERIAL WAR MUSEUM

From St Paul's a variety of buses can be used to get to Lambeth, via Blackfriars Bridge or Waterloo Bridge. St George's Circle is the readiest alighting point. From there down Lambeth Road to the museum. From St Paul's underground the smallest number of changes are one stop eastbound on the Central Line to Bank, then southbound on the Northern Line to The Elephant & Castle. From here, a walk up St George's Road to the museum.

Above: A view of the aviation gallery at the Imperial War Museum. 'Flying' left to right are Fw 190, P-51D Mustang and Spitfire I. In the foreground the top wing of a Zeppelin-killing Sopwith Camel and the nose cone of a Polaris missile.
Below: The cockpit of Lancaster I DV372 'Old Fred', proudly showing off its 49 sortie tallies at Lambeth. Close inspection is possible, revealing the cramped conditions in which the crew had to work.
Both Paul Shaw

The Imperial War Museum charts the history of warfare in the 20th century and therefore aviation is but one constituent in a large remit. The aviation gallery displays seven complete airframes, a Royal Aircraft Factory BE.2, a Sopwith Camel 2F1, Supermarine Spitfire I, North American P-51D Mustang, Heinkel He 162A-1 Salamander, a Focke-Wulf Fw 190A-8 and a Fieseler Fi 103 – better known as a V-1 'Doodlebug'. (The BE.2 was built by Ruston, Proctor & Co in Lincoln, see Trail G.) There are three cockpit sections, an Avro Lancaster I, a Handley Page Halifax A.VII and a Mitsubishi A6M 'Zero'. The Halifax is a 'walk-through' exhibit, while taking everything in, a sound track of a crew over a target in Germany can be heard. A platform against the Lancaster nose offers a unique chance to look down in the cockpit. Heady stuff!

With a large number of military exhibits, special exhibitions, a cinema and numerous displays, there is always much to take in. More details on admissions, exhibitions etc on 0171 4165320.

## SCIENCE MUSEUM

(Two options within the tour to route to the Science Museum have already been given, otherwise now is the time to cross the river and visit.) There are several options by bus, including retracing the steps given above back to the Strand and then taking services through Trafalgar Square and Piccadilly Circus for the Albert Hall. The Science Museum is behind the Albert Hall, reached down Exhibition Road. For the underground, from Lambeth North or the Elephant & Castle go northbound on the Bakerloo Line to the Circle & District Line at the Embankment and go westbound to South Kensington. The Science Museum is reached by walking north up Cromwell Place and into Exhibition Road, it is behind the Natural History Museum.

**Displayed within the Science Museum is Hawker P.1127 XP831, which made its first (tethered) hover on 21st October 1960 and went on to father the spectacularly successful Harrier. BAe**

The new and impressive 'Flight' gallery at the Science Museum involved considerable planning to get all the exhibits in. Largest whole airframe exhibit is HS.125 Series 1 executive jet G-ASSM. The picture gives a clue to how it was all done! Science Museum

For the Science Museum, aviation is only a part of this enormous venue. For aviation enthusiasts, this is a mecca of aviation heritage, through to the latest technology presented in the form of the 'Flight Lab' area where all ages can try the principles of flight 'hands on'. More details on 0171 9388080. The Cody Biplane is the first aircraft to have entered a British museum. Used in the military manoeuvres of 1912, it was presented to the museum in 1913 with only 2½ flying hours.

Of the other airframes here, many stand out: A V Roe;s second Triplane which first flew on 13th July 1909; Leon Levavasseur's Antoinette monoplane of 1910; Alcock and Brown's trans-Atlantic Vickers Vimy IV; Amy Johnson's Gipsy Moth; the Schneider trophy-winning Supermarine S.6B along with Jacques Schneider's magnificent trophy. Of the jet age there is Britain's first jet aircraft, the Gloster E28/39 along with an example of the Whittle W1 engine, the prototype Hawker P.1127 'jump jet' and an HS.125 executive jet, whose dimensions permit it to stand in for a full-blown jetliner. A cutaway section of a Boeing 747 fuselage, complete with seats, shows the impossibility of displaying any more of this monster. There is a diverse array of artefacts, models, components, engines, uniforms and diaramas.

**To return to Westminster:** Bus routes via Piccadilly Circus and Trafalgar Square. Underground from South Kensington to Westminster eastbound on the District & Circle Line.

**Diversions:** There are other attractions in London which may be of interest to the military minded:

HMS *Belfast*, 11,500 tonnes Second World War cruiser, now a floating museum moored near Tower Bridge, access from Morgan's Lane, off Tooley Street. (0171 4076434)

Museum of Artillery, Woolwich. Exhibits include an Auster AOP.9 'eyes for the guns'. (0181 3165402)

National Army Museum, Royal Hospital Road, SW3. (0171 7300717)

National Maritime Museum, Greenwich. A great maritime collection showing life at sea from the days of Drake and Nelson onwards. (0181 8584422)

Royal Air Force Museum, Hendon. Requiring no introduction to readers! (0181 2052266)

Royal Naval College, Greenwich. (0181 8582154).

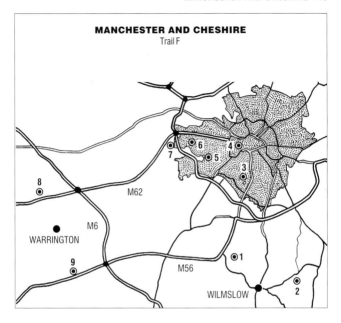

**MANCHESTER AND CHESHIRE**
Trail F

1   Manchester Airport
2   Woodford
3   West Didsbury
4   Museum of Science
    and Industry
5   Trafford Park
6   Eccles
7   Barton
8   Burtonwood
9   Stretton

This tour is in contrast to the others in that it spends time in an industrial conurbation and not in idyllic countryside. But that is the very essence of the major contribution this area gave to the war effort. It gave its industrial muscle and skill, for it is here that the RAF got the majority of its Lancasters. Woodford was the home of Avro (and still is, now that the name has resurfaced) and was also the assembly point for Metropolitan-Vickers.

I have included the site of the 'Metro-Vick' factory in Trafford Park in this trail because, like myself, you may have seen photographs of Lancaster sections on lorries. I went along to associate the backdrop of the photographs with the factory. Alas, much has been demolished along Mosley Road and the buildings along Westinghouse Road were due for demolition. (There were others who built fine aircraft in Manchester, Fairey at Heaton Chapel and Hills also in Trafford Park.) I was sorry I was unable to find a memorial or plaque to mark the contribution made here.

A successful repair to the grave of John Alcock will leave one unaware that the propeller blades once stood proud of the plinth. Along with Arthur Whitten Brown, Alcock took 16 hours and 12 minutes to cover 1,800 miles of Atlantic Ocean in 1919. How long did the vandals take to break the tips off the propellers? These dregs of modern society further enhance my view of men as outstanding as John Alcock and lift to a point of incredulity my perception of their courage and achievements.

## MANCHESTER AIRPORT

*Junction 5 of the M56 for the main terminal entrances. 'South side' and the viewing area are off the A538 (Junction 6 of the M56) under the runway and left on the road to Styal.*

During the Second World War – and to many today – known as Ringway and closely associated with the Parachute Regiment. When a recruit had done his 'Hardwick' (see Trail J), he came to Ringway for his parachute training and many were the unwary who 'Rang the bell'.

Ringway became Manchester Airport in June 1938, but the coming war largely took over events. Now it is Britain's second busiest airport and aiming for further expansion. Within the terminal area are many reminders of the past. Former RAF buildings survive, including the Station HQ, decontamination centre, NAAFI, messes and barrack blocks. (These buildings are detailed in *British Airfield Buildings of the Second World War* – see page 125.)

Outside the Airport Police building is a sculpture commemorating the achievements of Alcock and Brown. A memorial to the Parachute Regiment is in the garden near Terminal A and a plaque to the memory of 613 (City of Manchester) Squadron is in Terminal B.

Manchester is a very busy airport where a day could be spent watching aircraft arrive and depart. This can be best done from a purpose-made area to the south of the airport. Brown tourist signs for 'Aviation Viewing Area' can be followed from the terminals, via the A538 Wilmslow road and under the tunnel carrying runway 06. Here can be had excellent views and there is a cafe, shops and toilet facilities.

The 'South Side' hangars at Manchester Airport, relics of its wartime days. Paul Shaw

Turn left out of the viewing area and into Moss Lane. This passes three hangars on what is known as the 'South Side' and many wartime buildings survive here. This is private property, but a good view can be gleaned. Further along can be found two public footpaths offering further views of the airport, but they are a long way from suitable parking.

## WOODFORD
8 miles 15 minutes.

*DIVERSION: From Manchester Airport terminal, rejoin the M56 westbound and leave at Junction 6, the A538 to Wilmslow. From the airport viewing area, retrace steps to the A538 Wilmslow road. Stay on the A538 through Wilmslow, under the bridge at Wilmslow station and then left on the A5102 to Dean Row and Poynton. The airfield is on the right.*

The geography of this trail means that Woodford is a diversion. It should be a place a pilgrimage, a place to feel a special aura, a place that creates a mental picture of a vast aerial armada, a place to relate present architecture to wartime photographs. But it is none of these things. It is a shy place, loathe to reveal itself to the public. A place where the buildings have had to advance with the size of its products. Apart from the annual airshow, there is no public access. The huge production sheds can be seen from the A5102 and there are fleeting views to be had of the airfield from this road. Best method to look on to the airfield is from the A523 Poynton to Prestbury road.

**Retrace steps to Manchester Airport** and rejoin the trail.

## WEST DIDSBURY
6 miles, 10 minutes

*Follow signs for Manchester using the M56, which then continues into the A5103. Under the M63 and at the first major junction turn left on the A5145 (signed Stretford and Eccles). A short distance on the right is the Southern Cemetery.*

Parking can be nearby, pass through the main gates on foot, go straight ahead at the main intersection and in a few yards is a circular area within which is the grave of John Alcock KBE, DSC. The stone propeller at the base commemorates the famed west-east Atlantic crossing in the Vickers Vimy on 15th June 1919. (The Vimy is on show in the Science Museum at South Kensington, London, Trail E.) The monument records the loss

Above: **Assembly of Vulcan B.1s on Woodford's massive production line, 1957. Ansons, Manchesters, Lancasters and Lincolns had all gone before.** British Aerospace

Below: **Now under the banner of Avro International Aerospace, Woodford's current project is also four-engined, but a very different animal, the highly successful Regional Jetliner series. RJ85s for Lufthansa CityLine awaiting delivery in late 1995. This bay is to the right of the Vulcans in the other illustration.** Avro Communications

The memorial to John Alcock in Manchester's Southern Cemetery. Paul Shaw

The museum has many aircraft on display and a wide range of artefacts. The theme is the history of flight and its impact on society and whenever possible, local products are used. Hence there is a predominance of Avro types, including the 504K, Avian, Shackleton and the 707A WZ736, part of a batch of small deltas designed to glean aerodynamic information for the Vulcan. WZ736 was assembled at Bracebridge Heath and flown from Waddington – more details in Trail G. Among the many other items on show are a series of beautifully carved wind tunnel models and a HS Trident jetliner cockpit.

Aviation is not the only aspect of the museum, the whole site being a fascinating visit, including the world's oldest railway station with a variety of locos and rolling stock, plus many other exhibits. (More details on 0161 8322244 or Manchester Tourist Information on 0161 2343157.)

of John Alcock while ferrying the prototype Vickers Viking amphibian G-EAOV to the Paris Aeronautical Exhibition – in weather his friends tried to dissuade him from flying in – on 18th December 1919. There is also a Polish Air Force memorial in the cemetery.

## MUSEUM OF SCIENCE & INDUSTRY
4 miles, 10 minutes

*Retrace the route to the A5103 and turn left for the city centre. The museum is well signposted along this route, follow the tourist brown signs. There is parking on site.*

## TRAFFORD PARK
4 miles, 10 minutes

*Follow signs for Old Trafford and then Trafford Park. Mosley Road is just north of Barton Dock Road (the B5211), close to Junction 4 of the M63.*

This industrial area was home to the Metropolitan-Vickers Electrical Company who built 944 Mk I and 136 Mk III Lancasters. The plant was located east of Mosley Road and south of Westinghouse Road. It was they who built R5868 which moved to Ringway for test and was ready for collection by the RAF on 20th June 1942. Initially serving with 83 Squadron at Scampton, Lincolnshire, by September 1943 she had 'S-Sugar' with 467

Passengers boarding Allied Airways DH Dragon Rapide G-ADAH Pioneer for a flight to Inverness in late 1938. One of several delightful full-scale dioramas at the Museum of Science and Industry in Manchester. Ken Ellis

Squadron, RAAF, at Bottesford, Leicestershire. In all, she made 137 sorties, the last one being to Flensburg on 23rd April 1945. Today, 'Sugar' is the centre-piece of the Bomber Command hall at the RAF Museum, Hendon, see Trail E.

Church Street, Eccles (pedestrianised, off the large island in the centre of Eccles off the A57), is a stained glass window in memory of the former cadets of 292 Squadron Air Training Corps, who served in the Second World War.

## ECCLES
2 miles, 5 minutes

*Use Barton Dock Road from the bottom of Mosley Road and travel straight on to cross the Manchester Ship Canal by Barton Bridge. Turn right into Barton Lane for the centre of Eccles.*

In the parish church of St Mary the Virgin in

## BARTON
2 miles, 5 minutes

*Follow A57 (signed Irlam) and M63 signs from Eccles. Under the M63 overpass and stay on the A57. The aerodrome is signed on the right.*

Barton aerodrome is a busy grass airfield with a thriving light aircraft population and is home to the Lancashire Aero Club. Opened

Above: **Imperial Airways Handley Page HP.42 G-AAXC *Heracles* outside the main hangar at Barton,
1932.** Ken Ellis collection
Below: **Barton's attractive control tower was built for the aerodrome's short-lived role as Manchester's
airport in 1930.** Ken Ellis

as Manchester's airport on 1st June 1930, air service were quite short-lived and the need for more space was focused on the site at Ringway. Fairey test flew Hendon bombers and later Battles from Barton and F Hills & Sons test flew Percival Proctors which had been built at Trafford Park. The large brick built hangar and the wonderful control tower are reminders of the aerodrome's 1930 start. The extended blister hangar near to the tower, while a genuine wartime example, is not original to the site.

Most weekends pleasure flights, both fixed and rotary winged, operate and there is a functional visitor centre. The Macclesfield Historical Aviation Society have a small collection of airframes that can be inspected at weekends.

## BURTONWOOD
18 miles, 35 minutes

*Retrace the route to Junction 2 of the M63 and follow signs for Liverpool, M62. Leave the M62 at Junction 9, signed Warrington, A49. At the first roundabout, take the A574 for Widnes. Ignore early signs for Burtonwood and take the fourth island, with the superstore on the corner, signed Burtonwood, 3 miles. Also ignore the signs for 'RAF Burtonwood', which is a huge US deep storage site, remote from the airfield and in the process of winding down. At the second traffic island, turn right, still following Burtonwood signs.*

The road goes over the M62 on a bridge just west of the Burtonwood services. Here can be found a commanding view of the former airfield, now bisected by the motorway. Looking west from the bridge, it can be seen

that this motorway has a very special 'hard shoulder', a small sliver of the runway can be seen before the motorway follows it exactly, thus avoiding hard-core cost for half a mile. Discoloration marked another runway while evidence of the third runway remains between the 'J' type and Lamella hangars located north of the motorway.

Burtonwood was a huge US base with the hangars and magnificent control tower forming a dramatic landmark to the south of the motorway. The original wartime tower was extant in front of its grand successor until the early 1970s. Burtonwood became a Base Air Depot in 1942 handling and maintaining the huge influx of aircraft required by the USAAF. Post-war it retained much of this role and became a major terminal for USAF transports until this duty was transferred to Mildenhall in 1958. All of the sprawling complex south of the M62 was demolished in the late 1980s.

(If readers are so moved, with the Marks & Spencer superstore, on the main staircase, is a plaque noting that the store was built on the east end of the main runway of the former base.)

## STRETTON
13 miles, 23 minutes

*Retrace the route from Burtonwood to the M62 and join it, eastbound. Join the M6 south and leave at Junction 20, following signs for Warrington. Almost immediately, turn left for Stretton, the B5356.*

No longer may the term 'airfield' be used at the former RNAS Stretton (HMS *Blackcap*) which lies against Appleton Thorn village. It is an oddity for so much to survive, yet totally

Surviving hangars to the north of the M62 motorway serve to remind visitors of the once vast facility at USAF Burtonwood; 'J' type (above) and Lamellas (below).

Below: Looking west from a bridge over the M62 motorway, a small stretch of Burtonwood's huge main runway can still be seen. All Paul Shaw

Top: **At its peak as a USAF gateway base, Burtonwood must have had miles of ramp space. The superb tower complex was built onto a 'J' type hangar in 1953, this photo taken circa 1980, not long before its downfall.** Aldon P Ferguson

Above: **Today's Stretton is very much bisected, but a lot remains to be seen. Both of the 'A1' hangars used for Barracuda assembly survive, compare with the photograph, right.** Paul Shaw

lose the adhesion needed to retain the 'feel' of an aerodrome. The main culprit is the M56 motorway which divides the former airfield into two.

Travelling toward Appleton Thorn on the B5356, five hangars can be seen on the left. As the road turns to the right, Lyncastle Way is on the right. This is the old perimeter track that is now the main road for the industrial estate. Leave the industrial estate and turn right, then turn right into Langford Way. This follows the line of one of the runways, although there are no indicators until near the M56, where there are two small sections of intersecting runway. Leave Langford Way by turning right to pass over the M56 by the first bridge to the west of the M6-M56 interchange. South of the M56 are two 'A1' hangars, which were originally used by Fairey to assemble and flight test Barracudas. Take the next right, heading towards Arley, and again the lane uses the perimeter track and an excellent view of the runway can be achieved. It is possible to thread the way through and return to Appleton Thorn, using the second bridge.

**To return to Manchester Airport**: Retrace steps to the M56 and travel eastbound, following signs for the airport.

96 H.M.S. BLACKCAP 18·4·45 500' 8" SOUTH

RNAS Stretton in April 1945, looking south. In the foreground are three Mainhill 'S' Sheds and beyond
the runway threshold to the right the two Fairey 'A1's. Aircraft visible include Chance Vought Corsairs,
Grumman Wildcats, North American Harvards, an Avro Anson and a Fairey Barracuda. via Dave Smith

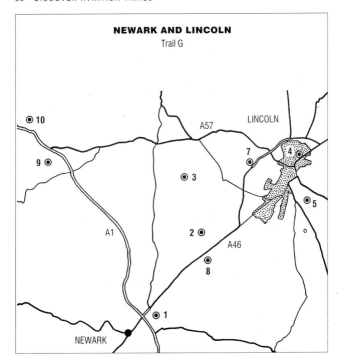

**NEWARK AND LINCOLN**
Trail G

1  Winthorpe
2  Morton Hall and
   'Norton Disney'
3  Wigsley
4  Lincoln Cathedral
5  Bracebridge Heath
6  Waddington
7  Skellingthorpe
8  Swinderby

To give a flavour of the area covered in this trail, I would say it is a piece of Old England. Newark with its pantile roofs is still a relatively compact market town that the progress of the 1960s was unable to touch. The villages also reflect the resistance, whether by accident or design, of the dormitory syndrome. A railway station with level crossing gates still opened and closed by hand looks unchanged from the war years. It is here that the siding would have been to accept munitions of war, including chemicals, for the nearby storage and filling site. Near such a place, one might dwell on the fact that an enemy had already shown that such potential retaliation was necessary.

Detractors of the worth of Bomber Command have denigrated the efforts of air and ground crew alike by applying a modern mind. These men were volunteers and did so willingly. Pilots expecting to be in fighters defending their homeland; navigators and air gunners hoping to be in Coastal Command defending their country's lifeline. Dwell not upon the policy the men of bomber Command were asked to execute, dwell upon the courage of these men – for you may well be passing over ground that many Victoria Cross holders have trod before you.

Lincoln would have undoubtedly seen such men, as it has seen so much of our history. It would be my wish for everyone to see Lincoln for the first time from afar, as I saw it. A gloomy day, travelling north along the Fosse Way. The clouds open enough to allow a shaft of sunlight to shine down upon the Cathedral city. On that same journey, to pass by old gates of a walled city and on northwards to pass by RAF Scampton where Lancaster NX611 once stood as gate guardian. Your introduction may not quite be the same, but your enjoyment of this area will.

## WINTHORPE

*Well signed off the A1, A46 and A17 just north east of Newark-on-Trent.*

The site of Newark Show Ground was that of the former RAF Winthorpe and the infrastructure of the airfield has been utilised. The three runways have survived, one is not too easy to define, one is fairly easy to discern despite obstructions and the third is obvious when used by the gliders of the Newark Gliding Club but not so when it is used as a car park!

Winthorpe is also home of the Newark Air Museum, situated on an old dispersal on the eastern edge of the airfield. This is an excellent – and expanding – museum with something for everyone. A wide selection of airframes are on display, both outside and inside the capacious 'new' aircraft display hall. There is a small section of fuselage from Lancaster I W4964 which gives a rare insight into the 'Lanc's' construction. (The Battle of Britain Memorial Flight's Lancaster carries the markings of W4964, 'WS-J' of 9 Squadron, the survival of a part of the original but a stone's throw away is a remarkable co-incidence. More of the BBMF in Trail D – East of Lincoln.)

The museum also boasts a Phantom flight simulator, an engine display hall and a host of other fascinating exhibits. The Newark Air Museum has something else of rarity to offer, depending on staffing levels – the chance to be inside the Hastings, Shackleton, Vulcan and, occasionally, the Varsity. To be able to clamber over the mainspar of the Shackleton – direct Lancaster lineage – is something special. For a small extra charge this is icing on an already plentiful cake. (Normally available on Sundays, but a telephone ahead is advised on 01636 707170.

Above: **A view of Newark Air Museum's aircraft display hall, shortly after completion. Aircraft, left to right, include: SE.5 replica, Jet Provost nose, Venom, Provost, Lancaster fuselage section, Sea Venom, Sea Hawk, Whirlwind, Sycamore, Skeeter, Sioux, Sycamore, Safir.** NAM

Below: **One of Newark's many 'star' exhibits is Vulcan B.2 XM594, which last served with 44 Squadron 'up the road' at Waddington. She flew into Winthorpe on 7th February 1983.** MAP

This will also bring details of opening times, admissions and special events.)

The museum's extensive shop can be visited without going into the museum, if you are so disciplined. A lovely place to browse, there is evidence too of the enthusiasm here with books on local aviation history written by members.

On leaving the museum, turn left towards Newark. Before the roundabout at the A46, the north east-south west runway can be seen crossing, and to the left the road to the indoor bowls club uses the perimeter track.

Turn left on to the A46, heading for Newark, beyond the bowls club is the base where a hangar stood. At the junction of the A46 and A17 is the threshold of the west-east runway. Turn left on the A17 signed for Sleaford and the other end of the north east-south west runway can be seen crossing the new road.

Further along, a farm track can be seen, this uses the old perimeter track and still links with the south east-north west runway. Turn left at the next junction and this road will complete the circuit of Winthorpe.

Looking back towards Newark will reveal a thin, shiny chimney near a squat brick tower. These are part of a ball bearing works that was in production during the war. Note the wartime buildings within the farm nearby. Winthorpe originally had grass runways, but when the metalled versions were laid, the risk to the ball bearing works was considered too great with 'heavies' taking off and landing – the north east-south west runway pointing directly at the works.

## MORTON HALL
8 miles, 15 minutes

*From the Newark Air Museum, join the A46 heading for Lincoln. An airfield will come into view on the right, this is the former RAF Swinderby, of which more later. At the crossroads with the 'Halfway Hotel' on the corner, turn left for Morton and Swinderby. Follow sings for the HM Borstal.*

Morton Hall was the home of 5 Group's headquarters following their move from St Vincent's in Grantham. The site is now a borstal and the old hall was demolished following a fire.

## 'NORTON DISNEY'
1 miles, 5 minutes

*From Morton Hall, turn left at the next junction, then turn right. Over the level crossing at Swinderby station and a short distance on the left.*

The large bomb dump used the cover of the woods for secrecy and for similar reasons the name of the village it carries has no bearing on the location. (Norton Disney itself lying to the south, the other side of the A46.)

The railhead for the dump was behind Swinderby station and little remains. It is possible to verify the site as a plot of land is still disused, just against the public road. This is about 500 yards on from the railway, marked by two big trees on the left. There is a loading ramp, concrete road, building bases, the remains of walls and piles of concrete. Two miles further on is Eagle Hall wood, and this remote place was used for the storage and filling of chemical weapons. The buildings and roads are still here, but out of sight from public gaze, although a small Nissen-like hut can be discerned. A modern sign at the gate still proclaims this to be a Ministry of Defence site within the meaning of the Official Secrets Act and is therefore emphatically out of bounds.

## WIGSLEY
3 miles, 8 minutes

*Head into North Scarle and beyond, then turn right to Wigsley.*

The road from Besthorpe to Wigsley passes over the edge of the former airfield, before the village that bears its name is reached. The perimeter track can be clearly seen and the path of one runway is crossed before reaching the control tower. A segment of the main runway can be found on the right following the control tower and the original concrete is visible when not covered with agricultural produce. The third runway ran parallel to the country lane, which itself was the perimeter track.

The area remains an open space without the re-instatement of hedgerows. Other than the tower, buildings do survive, but only on the dispersed sites. The tower is of great interest, being a three-storey affair. Across the road from the tower are a number of blast shelters, behind which are the bases of buildings which formed the technical site.

## LINCOLN
11 miles, 25 minutes

*From Wigsley village to Harby and then Saxilby, joining the A57 just south of the town. Head into Lincoln. Follow the brown tourist signs for the Castle and Cathedral from Lincoln's ring road. There are car parks at the Lawn Visitor Centre and near the Castle.*

A city of great history, including being a major Roman enclave. Lincoln's link with aviation has been strong since the First World War, when it was among the five top producers of aircraft. The surrounding airfields were at the forefront of RAF history and the Cathedral acts as a focal point for these memories. Visible from a far away as Ludford Magna. the Cathedral remains a strong image in the minds of men who have seen Lincoln from the air.

St Michael's Chapel in the Cathedral has four memorial windows and houses the books of remembrance for 1 and 5 Groups with the names of 25,611 men who lost their lives from the local airfields. A service is held every Thursday at 10.30am.

Lincoln Castle is close to the Cathedral and deserves a visit to walk the battlements which give fine views over the city. On the opposite side of the Castle from the Cathedral is the Lawn Visitor Centre which includes a museum opened in 1995 on 50 and 61 Squadrons who flew from Skellingthorpe. This is mainly a photographic display, but includes items of memorabilia including paybooks, logbooks, escape artefacts and medals.

Nearby is the Museum of Lincolnshire Life which takes in all of the diverse activities of the county. A First World War Mk IV tank is on display.

**The Bomber Command memorial window inside Lincoln Cathedral.** Paul Shaw

(Details of opening times etc for venues in Lincoln from their Tourist Information Office on 01522 529828.)

After some or all of these delights have been sampled, walk down Steep Hill to Lincoln's shopping centre. (For those who have difficulty with this very steep, cobbled, walk, relocate the car to the many car parks at the foot of the hill.) Steep Hill leads straight into High Street and go under Stone Brow, a late 15th or early 16th century gateway.

On the left is where the 'Saracen's Head Hotel' was, the building now being a row of shops. A plaque mounted high on the wall notes the site of this famed wartime 'watering hole'. (More details can be found in the companion volume, *Aeronautical Pubs & Inns of Britain*.)

Walk along the north bank of the River Witham and cross Broadgate into Waterside North. It was here that the steam farm machinery factory of Clayton & Shuttleworth produced aircraft, including Handley Page 0/400 bombers and Sopwith Camel and Triplane fighters, from 1917. The family name of Shuttleworth is one and the same as that given to the collection at Old Warden in Bedfordshire.

About turn and turn left at Melville Street. Before crossing the Pelham railway bridge a large blue building can be seen on the left. This was the site of Ruston, Proctor and Company. They built BE.2s and Sopwith 1½ Strutter general purpose military aircraft and 1,575 Sopwith Camel fighters. BE.2c 2699, on show at the Imperial War Museum at Lambeth in London (see Trail E), was built here.

Over Pelham Bridge is Canwick Road. There is housing on one side, on the other was the factory of Robey & Company who built Sopwith 'Gunbus' fighters and Short 184 torpedo-carrying floatplanes.

# BRACEBRIDGE HEATH

7 miles, 15 minutes

*Follow the signs out of Lincoln for the A15 and Sleaford. Travel up the steep escarpment and after the A607 turns off to the right (signed RAF Waddington) the warehouses on the left close to the road can be seen to be hangars.*

The site here began life as the airfield of Robey & Company, becoming 4 Aeroplane Acceptance Park in 1917. The warehouse with its concertina-like doors is a Coupled General Service Shed, more commonly known by its form of construction, a 'Belfast Truss' hangar. During the Second World War it was used by Avro to refurbish Lancasters and post-war to assemble two of the Avro 707 aerodynamic test aircraft for the Vulcan. All aircraft were towed along the A15 to nearby Waddington for flight test, the flying field at Bracebridge not having been used since 1920.

# WADDINGTON

*Continue down the A15 for an unrestricted view of the airfield and the newly-opened WAVE.*

WAVE stands for Waddington Aircraft Viewing Enclosure, which was opened to the public on 30th March 1996. With shop, a cafe and toilet facilities this is a most welcome development allowing the comings and goings of this busy base to be seen to great advantage, without gumming up the A15, as has been the case in the past.

Currently based at Waddington, and using the huge modern hangar to the north are 8

Above: The 'Belfast Truss' hangars at the former Bracebridge Heath airfield still serve as warehousing and a centre for light industry. Ken Ellis

Below: Avro 707C WZ744 was one of two assembled at Bracebridge Heath (the other was 707A WZ736) and flown from nearby Waddington, in this case on 1st July 1953. Both are extant, WZ736 in Manchester (see Trail F) and WZ744 at the Aerospace Museum, Cosford. MAP

**Boeing Sentry AEW.1s are the main residents at Waddington.** Boeing

**General view across the northern part of Waddington, towards the huge hangar that houses the RAF's AWACS fleet.** Ken Ellis

and 23 Squadrons combining to operate the fleet of Boeing Sentry AEW.1 airborne warning and control system (AWACS). Aircraft using the British Aerospace operated Air Combat Manoeuvring Instrumentation range operate out of Waddington and a wide array of fighter types from all over Europe and beyond drop in.

Waddington has had an illustrious past originating in 1916, but it is forever associated with the Avro 'heavies', the Lancaster and the Vulcan. The gate guardian Vulcan B.2 XM607, which bombed Port Stanley on 1st May 1982 in a 4,000 miles, 15½ hour sortie can be seen from afar from the A15, but being within the camp, cannot be inspected close-up without prior permission.

Retrace steps to the junction in Bracebridge Heath and turn south on the A607, signed for Waddington and RAF Waddington. At the crossroads in the village stands the 'Wheatsheaf' public house which has a number of aviation prints within. On the opposite corner is a set of shops at the far end of which is a memorial clock to 463 and 467 Squadrons, both Australian units that flew Lancasters out of Waddington 1943-45 until moving on to Skellingthorpe. The clock stands outside the cemetery where airmen of the Royal Flying Corps are to the right and those of the Second World War to the left.

At the next cross roads, turn right into the village centre. Here is the attractive 'Horse & Jockey' public house, within which are aviation photographs and prints, one of which depicts Waddington in 1917.

**Diversion**: Continue down the A607 to Navenby for the 'Lion & Royal' and the Navenby Heritage Room and on to the former Wellingore airfield (for both see Trail D). Return either by retracing up the A607, or via the A15

## SKELLINGTHORPE
8 miles, 20 minutes

*From Waddington retrace the route to Lincoln on the A15. Descend the escarpment and turn left at the junction, signed Newark A1434 (A46). After about a mile turn right into Rookery Lane at the 'Wagon and Horses'. Straight ahead into Skellingthorpe Road and stay straight ahead at the crossroads with Tritton Road. Continue over the railway crossing and pass the Hartsholme Country Park, with its lake, on the left. Turn left into Birchwood Avenue.*

The feel of the aerodrome has gone at the former RAF Skellingthorpe, but enough remains to identify the area. Once into Birchwood Avenue, opposite the junction, concrete bases remain marking what was the No 5 WAAF accommodation site. Continue along Birchwood Avenue, which was the main entrance to the station. Turn left into Fulmar Road, where the guardroom would have been. Further down is an electricity sub-station which occupies the very same site as its wartime counterpart. In the area against and behind the scout hut can be found evidence of the technical site with concrete roads and building bases. Within the community centre playing field, part of the perimeter track is used as a car park. In front of the community centre itself is a memorial to 50 and 61 Squadrons.

Next right is Jasmin Road, and the Lancaster Infant School. The majority of the roads here are named after RAF stations. Continue to the junction with Woodfield Avenue and turn left. On the outside of a sweeping left hand bend, trees mark remnants of the perimeter track and a runway end, a small section of which is extant.

Park outside St Hughes' Primary School. Face the school and walk along the footpath to the left until the corner of the wood is reached. A brick structure with a concrete roof was a blast shelter alongside the radar workshops. Straight ahead is a concrete circle in pristine condition, here the airfield controller's caravan was positioned. Other blast shelters are nearby and evidence of other dispersals and perimeter track. Now, back to the car...

Continue along Woodfield Avenue. The next school is named after Pilot Officer Leslie Manser who won the Victoria Cross on the '1,000 bomber' raid (Operation MILLENNIUM) on Cologne during the night of 30th/31st May 1942 flying Avro Manchester L7301 'ZN-D' of 106 Conversion Flight (but on loan to 50 Squadron) out of Skellingthorpe. There is a silhouette of a Lancaster incorporated into the school sign.

Wend through to the large traffic island on Lincoln's ring road (the A46) and turn right, towards Lincoln. Along this road there are two footpath signs before the bend and they mark the former Skellingthorpe bomb dump, features of which can still be identified. Park in the lay-by and traces can be found on both sides of the road, but predominantly on the northern side.

Two bomb stores are in good condition, one in poor shape, plus a pyrotechnic and incendiary store, another bomb store (Type 5416) and a component store. Two fusing points can be identified by the long narrow roads and earthen blast walls.

Continue to the next traffic island and turn left for Skellingthorpe itself. At the community centre is a memorial and a heritage room, which shows the history of the airfield and other aspects of the area.

(More details of the heritage room on 01522 529828.)

## SWINDERBY

5 miles, 7 minutes

*Retrace the route to the Lincoln ring road and turn to Newark on the A46. Continue on the A46 until the 'Halfway House' is passed on the right. At the next crossroads, turn left, at a sign marked Camp Road. The former Swinderby airfield is on either side of the road.*

Closed in 1995 and for disposal as this was written, Swinderby not surprisingly is well preserved. All of the station buildings remain, the runway and adjacent perimeter track are in perfect condition. Two other runways are extant, but not in the best of health. There are three 'J' type hangars and three 'T2s'. All can be seen with ease from public roads.

The 'Halfway House' public house on the A46 contains aviation photographs and squadron plaques. The museum in the Lawn Visitor Centre in Lincoln has an interesting sequence of photographs taken from the same angle showing Swinderby since its earliest days.

**Swinderby to Winthorpe:** Retrace the route to the A46 and turn south west for Newark. At the junction with the A1133, the Newark air Museum is signed on the left. (6 miles, 8 minutes)

**Diversion:** Polish Air Force Cemetery can be found off London Road, Newark and includes the Polish Air Force and Warsaw Air Bridge Memorials. This is on the Newark to Balderton road (the B6326) and is marked with brown tourist signs. Note that the brown signs point through the main gates, but it is easier to use Elm Avenue down the side of the cemetery.

## OSSINGTON
11 miles, 20 minutes

*DIVERSION: From Newark join the A1 northbound and leave at the signs for Carlton and Sutton-on-Trent. Turn left for Ossington.*

The public road from Ossington to Kneesall crosses the old airfield by using a section of runway to an intersection with another which it then uses. Other runways have been removed, but the perimeter track remains in its entirety but is on private land, as indeed is the whole airfield. Dispersals survive, but cannot be seen from the public road. The WAAF accommodation site (on the Moorhouse road) has the only wartime buildings extant.

## RETFORD AIRPORT
12 miles and 20 minutes

*DIVERSION: Follow signs to Tuxford and join the A1 northbound. The airfield lies between the B6387 and a minor road linking Elkesley and Ordsall.*

Abandoned in 1957, RAF Gamston has seen a renaissance and is now Retford Airport, with much investment in new hangars and a modern control tower/admin block. Runway 21/03 is active, although another is used by the gliders of the Dukeries Gliding Club at weekends.

The whole of the perimeter track remains, part of which has been resurfaced to serve the industrial estate which sits between the A1 and the airfield. Many wartime buildings remain on the industrial estate as does the original control which has been turned into a dwelling. The airfield is best surveyed from the Elkesley to Ordsall road on the western boundary.

**To return to the Newark Air Museum:** In both cases, retrace steps to the A1 and go southbound to Newark, to the A46 junction, then following signs for the Newark Air Museum.

Light aircraft parked in front of the new control tower and hangar block at Retford Airport, the former RAF Gamston. Ken Ellis

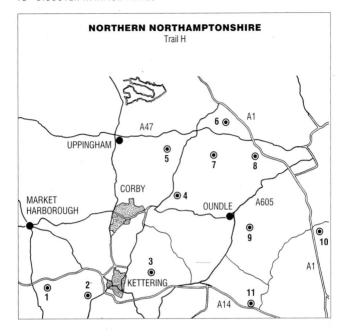

## NORTHERN NORTHAMPTONSHIRE
### Trail H

1  Harrington
2  Great Cransley
3  Grafton Underwood
4  Deenethorpe
5  Spanhoe Lodge
6  Wittering
7  King's Cliffe
8  Sibson
9  Polebrook
10 Glatton
11 Molesworth

It is clear from the memorials in North-amptonshire that the people of the county had an impact on the Americans as much as the Americans had an impact on the people of Northamptonshire. The memorials reflect the mutual admiration and respect that still exists today.

It is little wonder that the Americans fell in love with 'little ol' England' when they saw this area. There is no need to wonder where the Americans found their motivation to rise to great deeds. It is still here to cherish and want to protect. People and a way of life, all the more valuable for the friendship enjoyed all those years ago.

It is not surprising that there is a special relationship, because the Americans are among their own kind here. They were pro-tecting the very places from where some of their ancestors came from. The family of George Washington came from Sulgrave, Great Brington, Thrapston and Islip, their coat of arms incorporates stars and stripes. Benjamin Franklin's father was born in Ecton before he sailed to America in 1683.

The sounds of the wartime can still be heard in this area from the Johnny Harris Band. They bring alive the melodies and atmosphere of a 1940s dance, on stage in United States Army Air Force (USAAF) uniforms and playing the Glenn Miller sound to perfection.

# HARRINGTON

*The museum is well signposted off the Harrington to Lamport road, (access via the long track adjacent and south of the A14) and Harrington is easily reached by using junction two when travelling east. When travelling west from the east (A1), use junction 4. (Junction 3 has restricted access).*

Until recently, it could be said that no buildings had survived, but following the recent opening of the 'Carpetbagger' Avia-tion Museum, it transpires that buildings are extant away from the public gaze. The museum uses the so-called 'bomb proof' administration building and the pay master's hut is used by the Northamptonshire Aviation Society to show off their many treasures they have recovered from the county's crash sites.

The 492nd and the 801st Bomb Groups were the only American nocturnal fliers in the European theatre of operations. Something unique, it is fitting that the 'Carpetbagger' Museum has found the right setting and presentation to give a flavour of the work carried out by these groups from Harrington. There is something else at the museum which is unusual. Some of the photographs of agents destined for enemy territory, who would have left Britain from Harrington, leave one with a knot in the stomach. This is from a real sense of sharing the apprehension and fear that must be only a hint of that which those courageous agents felt, all those years ago on this very airfield. (More details of the museum on 01604 686608.)

Very little remains of this airfield and yet, those remains are such that an entertaining time can be enjoyed piecing them together, to form a whole image in one's mind. The

Evocative shot of a 'Carpetbagger' B-24 Liberator taking off from Harringworth's west-east runway with a supplies, or agents, for dropping into occupied Europe. This imagery has been used on today's memorial and the cottages in the background are still to be seen. via Ron Clarke

Memorial to the 801st and 492nd BG 'Carpetbaggers' at Harrington. Paul Shaw

remains of the RAF's Thor ballistic missile sites are in the centre of an area that retains an open feeling in wonderful countryside, surrounded by a good deal of perimeter track, interspersed with clues only to the runways.

On leaving the museum, turn right from the long access road toward Lamport. At the T-junction with the B576, turn right. In only a short way, the memorial stands a little back form the road, behind a fence on the left. The image of a black Liberator taking off, with a row of cottages in the background, can be seen on the memorial. One has only to walk a few steps along the perimeter track behind the memorial, to see those very same cottages.

Continue and take the next right turn to Draughton. Note the floor of the council compound on the corner, as this was the end of a runway. The lane to Draughton has been heavily disguised by nature to conceal that it was once the perimeter track. Original concrete and drains can still be found along the verges on each side of the road. At the sign marking the bridleway to Harrington, the old perimeter track can be seen to swing off to the right. A short way off the lane, the lie of the concrete reveals the start point and direction of another runway.

The bridleway offers the opportunity to follow the remaining half width concrete perimeter track, which can take one back to the museum. A word of caution, the bridleway is poorly signed close to the museum and it is therefore easier to use the bridleway onto the perimeter track from the museum.

There are aerial photographs of Harrington airfield within the museums. So it is possible to enjoy the challenge of the airfield with confirmation after, or enjoy relating the airfield to the photographs after visiting the museums.

(A phonetic clash of names meant that 'Harringworth' became Spanhoe Lodge to prevent lorries and airmen arriving at the wrong location – see page 79.)

## GREAT CRANSLEY

5 miles, 11 minutes

*Take the B576 towards Lamport. Turn left on to the minor road signed Old and Walgrave. In Old, follow signs for Broughton and join the A43 towards Kettering. Great Cransley is signed on the left, abeam Broughton.*

Within St Andrews church in the village of Great Cransley is the stained glass memorial known as the American Window. This was the gift of American servicemen from the 384th Bombardment Group, Grafton Underwood. They came to join the church services and were so taken by their welcome, they wanted to repay the kindness that had been shown.

Services were broadcast to America from here and a telegram of congratulations from America is on the pillar near to the memorial book. The window was dedicated on 6th May 1944 and a memorial book contains the names of those who contributed to the cost and attended the service of dedication. The window is in the bell tower, hidden by curtains, one has to look up steeply to see it. The flags of both nations are still to be seen and have never been moved since that day. This is a church that is always kept locked, details of where the key can be found are displayed on the church notice board.

B-17G Flying Fortress *Screaming Eagle* of Grafton Underwood's 545th Bombardment Squadron, 384th Bombardment Wing.

B-17Gs of the 384th 'at work'. Both Ken Ellis collection

## GRAFTON UNDERWOOD

11 miles, 19 minutes

*From Great Cransley, follow signs for Broughton and join the A43 to Kettering. Join the A14 westwards and leave at the next exit for A43, Corby and Stamford. In Geddington, follow the brown tourist signs for Boughton House. Pass by Boughton House and the site of Grafton Underwood is at the top of the rise.*

The first and last bombing missions over Europe by the USAAF were conducted from Grafton Underwood. A memorial on the path of where a runway used to be makes note of this prestigious fact. In keeping with this unique position, there are three special tributes to the past.

There is the memorial on the site of the old runway. The paths of the removed runways are defined by trees that are each dedicated to singular persons, or groups by persons or groups who wish to remember them. All these people are recorded in the porch of the church along with details of the location of each tree.

The third tribute is a beautiful hidden stained glass memorial window depicting a B-17 Flying Fortress in simple bold colours, within the church of St James the Apostle in Grafton Underwood village. The village itself appears unchanged, a beautiful and quiet place that needed the ugliness and noise of war to protect it.

A few wartime buildings remain, including the partially hidden battle headquarters that is only a few yards from a public road. There is not a strong 'feel' of an aerodrome here, despite the many blatant clues, yet strangely, there are many features that are readily recognised on archive film.

## WELDON

8 miles, 12 minutes

*Retrace the route from Grafton Underwood to Geddington. At the junction with the A43, turn right for Corby and Stamford. On the outskirts of Corby, not far past the junction with the A6116, turn right at the sign for Weldon.*

In the village of Weldon, in Church Street, is the Norman Church of St Mary the Virgin. Within is a stained glass memorial window donated by the men of the 401st Bombardment Group who were stationed at nearby Deenethorpe. Some of the panels in the window came from the Deenethorpe aerodrome chapel. This is another church that, of necessity, has to remain locked. The window can easily be seen from outside, but as ever, is so much better when viewed from within.

## DEENETHORPE

2 miles, 3 minutes

*With Weldon church on the left, leave Church Street. At the T-junction with the A427 turn right for Oundle.*

This is very much an airfield, with the provision of runway 04/22 being 3,000 x 75 feet surfaced in asphalt. Used by light aircraft and microlights, entrance to the flying area is off the A427 Weldon to Oundle road, but prior permission is required as this is a private operation. The control tower, long derelict, was demolished in the spring of 1996 because of persistent vandalism. A reduced width perimeter track and east to west runway survive, along with four spectacle

**The stained glass window in the church of St James the Apostle in Grafton Underwood.** Paul Shaw

dispersals. The operations block part of the technical site and domestic sites survive, the large majority of which is on private land. The minor road from Deene-thorpe to Upper Benefield offers little in the way of extra vantage points to the airfield.

A memorial by the side of the A427 is not backward in coming forward, it proudly states that the 401st Bombardment Group were 'The best damned outfit in the USAAF'. The site of this memorial used to enable the photographer to capture the memorial with the control tower in the background which made for a cracking good photo for those that had the opportunity!

A view that is no longer possible. The memorial to the 401st BG at Deenethorpe overlooks the airfield and it was possible to 'capture' the control tower in the view. The tower was demolished in the spring of 1996. Paul Shaw

## UPPER BENEFIELD
1 miles, 2 minutes

*Continue along the A427 toward Oundle and the 'Wheatsheaf' is on the right, within the village of Upper Benefield.*

'The Wheatsheaf' hotel, Upper Benefield, near Oundle was a favourite wartime haunt of American airmen, so much so, that visitors can enjoy a pint in the 401 Bar. There are photographs on the walls and memorabilia to be seen. (More details in the sister publication *Aeronautical Pubs and Inns of Britain*, see page 127.)

## SPANHOE LODGE
8 miles, 15 minutes

*Retrace the route along the A427 to the A43. Turn right on to the A43 toward Stamford, follow the left turn for Deene at the brown tourist sign for Deene Park and Kirby Hall. At the next junction, continue straight on for Harringworth and Seaton. At the next T-junction give way and the Spanhoe memorial and old aerodrome entrance is directly opposite.*

A little of the technical site remains along with some of the perimeter track. The majority of the airfield was lost through quarrying. The perimeter track that linked the south west-north east and south east-north west runways is used as a runway by the resident light aircraft.

Buildings that remain are to the south of this runway and include the motor transport wing. There are no original hangars extant although those erected by the thriving aircraft maintenance and restoration and paint and finishing businesses are very much in keeping. Needless to say, this area is to be regarded as operational and prior permission is required to visit, but a series of footpaths

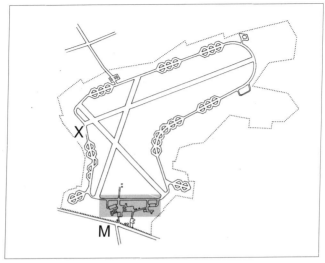

Above: **The airfield layout of Spanhoe Lodge, with its extensive dispersals. The existing Spanhoe aerodrome is shown shaded. The memorial is marked 'M'.** Pete West / Lincoln Graphics
Below: **Much of the north western part has been destroyed through extensive quarrying. A surviving single section of perimeter track stops in mid air on the western boundary of Spanhoe (marked 'X' on the map above.** Ken Ellis

do allow closer inspection of a good proportion of the surviving structures.

A memorial to the 315th Troop Carrier Wing, who flew Douglas C-47 Skytrains, stands at the old airfield entrance. There is a display board in the 'White Swan' public house in Harringworth village which records that period in words and photographs, again more details in our *Pubs* companion.

(Originally known as Harringworth, from the nearest village, the airfield took up the name of a local farm and wood, to avoid confusion with the more established Harrington, home of the 'Carpetbaggers' – see above. Harringworth or Spanhoe is also often called Wakerley, after another nearby village!)

road used by RAF vehicles, this was part of the perimeter track for the former RAF Collyweston, which was absorbed into the greatly enlarged Wittering in 1945-46. A journey up the A1 northbound goes past the main gate with its Harrier GR.3 'guardian' and views of the main Gaydon-type hangars.

Use the roundabout immediately after the base to turn around and come south. Leave the A1 at the junction with the A47 and turn westbound for Leicester, before quickly turning left into Wansford. (Here there is an option for yet another diversion, to Sibson – see below.) Follow the minor road to King's Cliffe and rejoin the trail and the memorial, which is on the left.

## WITTERING
10 miles, 12 minutes

*DIVERSION: From Spanhoe follow signs for Laxton and Blatherwycke. At the A43 turn north, signed Stamford. At the junction with the A47 turn east, signed Peterborough. After a right hand bend, the airfield will appear on the left with views possible for the next three miles. (From Harringworth, follow signs for Wakerley and Duddington to join the A43.)*

To the north east lies RAF Wittering, home of the Harrier 'jump jet'. A large and busy base, the Harrier GR.7s and T.10s of 1 and 20(R) Squadrons are resident. Best views of the airfield are from the A47. After the right hand bend on the A47 to the left will be seen what was the bomb dump from the days when Wittering was a 'V-Bomber' base. Between the bomb dump and the A47 can be seen a

## KING'S CLIFFE
7 miles, 18 minutes

*Leave Spanhoe by way of Laxton. Through Laxton, follow signs for Blatherwycke which is on route for King's Cliffe, where upon signs for Wansford should be followed.*

Pride of place against the former airfield of King's Cliffe, is the memorial using the shape of the wings of a North American P-51 Mustang and a Supermarine Spitfire. A memorial in these parts is not the end of efforts to remember. During celebrations for the 50th anniversary of VJ day, the flags were flying in style at this memorial. Towards Wansford can be found a spot to gain a distant view of the skeletal control tower. Toward King's Cliffe, a public footpath gives access to some sophisticated dispersals with revetments and blast shelters.

**The impressive memorial at King's Cliffe, the shape of the wings illustrating the different usage of the airfield during the Second World War.** Paul Shaw

Spitfires were the first aircraft to be based when King's Cliffe opened as a satellite of neighbouring Wittering in 1941 with 266 Squadron moving in. From December 1942 USAAF units began to arrive, but it was not to be until the following August that US occupation really got into full swing and the first Lockheed P-38H Lightnings of the 20th Fighter Group flew in. They were replaced by Mustangs in July 1944.

### SIBSON
7 miles, 12 minutes

*DIVERSION: Continue into Wansford and turn right on to the B671 for Elton. Sibson is clearly marked on the left.*

The attractive grass aerodrome at Sibson is now the home of an aero club and a parachute school. Other than the 'T2' type hangars and outbuildings, little remains of its wartime days on the aerodrome site.

Opened in mid-1940 as a satellite to RAF Peterborough (or Westwood), the airfield hosted many different types of trainer during its career to 1946. Visitors may be amazed to hear that aircraft the size of Vickers Wellingtons occasionally flew in and out of Sibson, but the wartime boundaries were larger than the present day aerodrome.

West of the B671 a whole series of wartime buildings now serve as a farm, in the latter years of RAF Sibson they were a repatriation camp.

**To rejoin the trail**, continue to Elton then turn right on to the A605 to Oundle.

## POLEBROOK

15 miles, 35 minutes

Polebrook's 351st BG 'Triangle J' tail marking forms the unit's memorial. Paul Shaw.

*There are a number of viable routes, the most scenic of which is by way of Apethorpe, Woodnewton and Fotheringay. Once on the A605 between Peterborough and Oundle, a black lorry route sign clearly points the way to Polebrook airfield.*

The old Polebrook airfield lies to the south of the Polebrook to Lutton Road. At the cross-roads with the Polebrook to Lutton road, the technical site is to the right and the sign for 351st BG (H) Memorial 8th Air Force is straight ahead toward Hemington.

In the main, runways and perimeter track have been removed except where areas have been isolated for agricultural storage. One such area has been cleared and at one end now stands a memorial to the 351st Bombardment Group who flew B-17 Flying Fortresses from the base.

An impressive memorial in its own right, the large expanse of extant runway serves to create a symbolic impression of the huge effort, of which Polebrook airfield played its part. Also on this site is a memorial seat to Lt General James T Stewart, commanding officer of the 351st's 508th Bombardment Squadron.

In the background is a 'J' type hangar with two warehouses occupying the plots of two wartime hangars. All three are part of the old technical site which has other surviving buildings.

As with Harrington (see above) architecture of another era is also to be found here, in the form of the launch pads and blast walls of 130 Squadron RAF's Thor ballistic missiles, which were stationed here from 1959 to 1963.

## GLATTON

9 miles, 20 minutes

*From Polebrook use a route of preference to the A1, ideally through Glatton. Stay on the A660 and cross the A1, follow signs for Peterborough Business Airfield (Conington)*

Home to the B-17 equipped 457th Bombardment Group, USAAF Station 130 took its name from the village of Glatton, and not the parish of Conington in which it lies. Today's aerodrome takes the latter name. With one of the runways (10/28) in use, this airfield is well worth a visit. A second runway (the wartime north west-south east) is easily seen, along with an adjacent perimeter track. The country lane linking Holme with Conington makes use of a section of the south west-north east runway. Kerbs have been placed along the section used as a road to reduce the width. North of this are the buildings of Red Court Farm which was surrounded by the runways, but allowed to 'trade' during the 457th's residency.

There is a memorial in Conington Church yard to the 457th Bomb Group. The only piece of evident airfield architecture, is the water tower against the A1.

Recent hangars and buildings close to the eastern threshold of the wartime east-west runway are occupied by Glatton's (Conington's) light aircraft. Ken Ellis

## MOLESWORTH
11 miles, 23 minutes

*Rejoin the B660 and head west, signed Kimbolton. Limited glimpses of the airfield can be had from Old Weston and beyond.*

Molesworth is readily identified by the enormous fence which surrounds this former airfield and current USAF base. The base came to fame in the mid-1980s when massive construction work changed the airfield structure with the erection of a mass of bunkers to house the Tomahawk cruise missiles of the 550th Tactical Air Missile Wing. These were withdrawn in 1989 when it could be said they had achieved their aim, without one of the hideous weapons being launched.

Inspection of the airfield is of course from afar, with a 'J' type hangar being viewed best from the B662. As might be expected, the now empty missile bunkers dominate.

**To return to Harrington:** Use the B660 to join the A14 westbound, signed Kettering. Leave the A14 at junction 4 and follow the A6 for Market Harborough. Turn left on to the B576 and follow signs for Harrington. In Harrington, join the Lamport Road, and the 'Carpetbagger' Museum is signposted just after the A14 is crossed. (22 miles, 35 minutes)

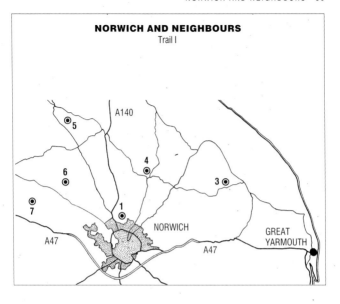

**NORWICH AND NEIGHBOURS**
Trail I

1  Norwich Airport
2  Rackheath
3  Ludham
4  Coltishall
5  Oulton
6  Swannington
7  Attlebridge

I have enjoyed the coastal resorts of Norfolk for many years and this trail gave me the motivation to see inland Norfolk. At the end of my day, I realised how much I had been missing. I travelled on Easter Bank Holiday weekend and it was most noticeable the advantages our hobby can bring. I endured the traffic in Norwich to drop the ladies off for the shops and through that popular location on the Norfolk Broads, Wroxham. I then revelled in the quietness of the airfields and the countryside they lie in.

The aircraft that graces the front cover, the English Electric Lightning gate guardian at RAF Coltishall was my first encounter with an airframe set on a plinth in such a dramatic and exciting pose. I thought it wonderful! (I hear it may not be there for much longer, a pity.)

There will be those who know Coltishall and will expect to see directions to the 'Three Horseshoes' in Scottow on the airfield's northern perimeter. Alas, all that could have been cherished has gone. For those like myself, who never had the chance to see everything, it seems to have been the kind of place where enthusiasts would have sat with a pint of water, in order to keep their senses sharp, while they took it all in. The pilot's signatures on the ceiling, the memorabilia, even what was alleged to be a Spitfire propeller on the outside wall. All has gone.

## NORWICH

Norwich is an enjoyable city, with the Cathedral, the old part of the town and the shops. Use of the 'Park and Ride' from Norwich Airport is recommended, although the city has ample parking.

Until a fire in 1994, there was a memorial room in the Central Library in Bethel Street to the memory of over 6,400 Americans of the 2nd Air Division (AD) who did not return home. It contained the rolls of honour along with books, material on American culture, historic papers and archives. It is a case of when, not if, the library and a new 2nd AD USAAF Memorial Room will be rebuilt.

A panel on the door of the City Hall shows a Boulton and Paul engineer at work on an aero engine and there are displays connected with the company in the Bridewell Museum. In the Cathedral, the standard of 97 Squadron has been laid up since disbandment at Watton on 2nd January 1967.

## NORWICH AIRPORT
3 miles, 12 minutes

*The airport is well signed out of the city centre, being to the east of the A140 Cromer road.*

Norwich Airport evolved from the airfield which was known as RAF Horsham St Faith. The station was operational until 1960, its last inmates being 74 Squadron on Hawker Hunter F.6s. There are two active runways with a third extant, but inactive. The whole of the perimeter track and dispersal survive, as do the hangars and many of the RAF buildings.

There is a memorial display to the 458th Bombardment Group (BG) within the terminal building. The 458th operated out of Horsham, flying Consolidated B-24 Liberators from January 1944 to April 1945. Nearby, within the 'Stakis Ambassador Hotel' there are plaques and photographs and the 'Wallbro Bar' is named after a pioneer Norfolk aircraft of 1910. A full-size replica Spitfire is on show in the courtyard. (More details of the Wallbro Monoplane in *Aeronautical Pubs & Inns in Britain*, No.3 in our Aviation Pocket Guide series.)

The City of Norwich Aviation Museum is on the northern edge of the airfield, with access of the A140 Cromer road. There is a large aircraft park, exhibits including a Vulcan B.2, Gloster Javelin FAW.9 and Meteor F.8. When staffing levels permit, it is possible to get into some of the airframes. There are extensive interior displays showing the RAF in Norfolk 1939-1945; Norfolk VCs; the 2nd Air Division and the 458th BG and Boulton and Paul production in Norwich. (More details on 01603 625309, or via Norwich tourist information on 01603 666071.)

## RACKHEATH
4 miles, 14 minutes

*From Horsham St Faith follow signs for Spixworth and then Rackheath. At the crossroads with the A1151, Norwich to Wroxham road, turn right for Norwich. From the 'Green Man', take the first left, signposted for Salhouse Station.*

There is no longer an airfield at Rackheath, but there is plenty to find. The road to Salhouse goes across the former airfield. One runway identifies itself in a short, full width, section and farm track width thereon.

Rackheath was home to the B-24 Liberator equipped 467th Bombardment Group, who were based at the airfield from February 1944 to April 1945.

**Diversion:** In the churchyard of Holy Trinity Church in nearby Plumstead (further south through Salhouse) is a memorial to the 467th BG and the village sign includes a B-24 image.

**The forlorn tower at Rackheath. Most of the wartime buildings are now crowded by the modern buildings of the industrial estate.** Paul Shaw

Backtrack now to the 'Green Man'. (This was a favourite haunt of Rackheath airmen, but today has only one aviation painting to show the connection.) On to the A1151 again, heading towards Norwich, take the second left, signed to the Industrial Estate. A sign immediately looms up for the USAAF Memorial.

The old technical site is an industrial estate and while the control tower, a hangar and other buildings survive, they do not assert themselves. The airfield atmosphere has been lost because of the congestion created by constructions around them. The memorial to the 467th BG, dedicated in 1990, followed this out-of-place feeling. In itself it is worthy, but the site does not stand out. There is a footpath from beneath the control tower which crosses the area of the old airfield, toward Salhouse railway station.

## LUDHAM
11 Miles, 30 minutes

*Follow the A1151 to Wroxham and take the right turn on to the A1062, signposted Ludham. Continue to Ludham village, take the left turn (on the bend), signposted Catfield. Turn right at the sign for Fritton and turn left at the next minor crossroads. If this turn is missed, it is very easy to navigate by public road around the airfield.*

Built as a satellite of Coltishall, Ludham has had a rich history its aircraft operating coastal strikes, sweeps into Europe and escort duties with based units predominantly operating Spitfires. The airfield has a very open atmosphere and very much retains the

'feel' of a wartime station. Part of the runway still functions as a landing strip and sections of perimeter track and a blister hangar can be found.

The control tower has been refurbished and forms the centre point for the Ludham Control Tower and War Museum, which includes a wide range of memorabilia. On display is the nose section of a Douglas B-26K Counter-Invader and a variety of vehicles. (More details on 01692 678251 or from Wroxham Tourist Information on 01603 782281.)

**Diversion:** Retracing steps westwards down the A1062 to Wroxham, bound for Coltishall, turn right off the A1062 at Horning, following the signposts for RAF Neatishead. The base itself, home to 83 and 432 Signals Units is very much a secure area. Prior permission is required to visit the base's 'guardian', McDonnell Douglas Phantom FGR.2 XV420. The Air Defence Battle Command & Control Museum and its associated 100 Group Museum hope to open up to the public during 1996 (more details from Wroxham Tourist Information on 01603 782281).

## COLTISHALL
16 miles, 30 minutes

*From Ludham back down the A1062 to Wroxham. At the crossroads with the A1151 in Wroxham, follow signs for Coltishall on the B1345.*

Coltishall is an attractive village by the River Bure which also gives its name to the airfield to the north. Coltishall is home to the RAF's Sepecat Jaguar fighter-bombers, operated by 6, 41 and 54 Squadrons.

**English Electric Lightning F.1A XM172 is a dramatic 'guardian' at the main entrance to Coltishall.**
Hugh Trevor

In Coltishall, follow signs for North Walsham on the B1150 and while still within the village, turn left just after crossing the railway bridge. Turn immediate right on to a single track road that passes Colk's Farm and ends up at Sudan Cottages. Here is a superb view across the airfield.

Retrace the route to the B1150 and turn left for North Walsham. Take the first left on the edge of Scottow. In the cemetery here, close to the runway threshold, many airmen are buried. Continue to the 'Give Way' signs, turn left followed by second left, following signs for RAF Coltishall.

On the main gate, posed dramatically is Lightning F.1A XM172 as a reminder of the days when Lightnings thundered in and out of Coltishall. Set within flower beds in front of the Station Headquarters, in 242 Squadron colours, is a full size replica of a Hawker Hurricane, 'V7467'. In June 1940 242's Hurricanes arrived here, under the command of Squadron Leader Douglas Bader. Both airframes are immaculately present in an attractive and well maintained environment.

Pride is the message here. Pride in themselves, pride in their achievements and in the equipment they use.

## OULTON
9 miles, 15 minutes

*Various routes to Oulton are viable from Coltishall. A suggestion: From Coltishall village take the B1354 signed to Aylesham. (This follows the track of the Bure Valley Railway and a stop at the old mill in Buxton is worthwhile.) At Buxton, turn left following signs for Cawston.*

Night Flying Equipment Store, one of several buildings that survive at Oulton, some of which now fulfil and new role.

The memorial at Oulton, recording the units based at the airfield: 18, 21, 88, 114, 139, 214, 223 and 236 Squadrons RAF, 1428 and 1699 Conversion Flights and the 803rd BG, USAAF. Both Ken Ellis

Photographs of the Fortress IIs and IIIs of 214 Squadron are rare, and air-to-airs more so. The poor quality of this view of 'BU-W' does not hide the large dorsal aerial amidships, or the under-nose radome. Peter Green collection

*At the intersection with the B1149 turn right, signed Holt. Take the second right for Oulton Street.*

The road to Oulton Street from the B1149 is on the fringe of the old airfield. Be sure also to use the byroad between Oulton Street and Oulton for a good view of the airfield. The runways and perimeter track survive here, though not completely. Much of the airfield site is covered in poultry houses and other farm buildings, and it may take time to establish the airfield layout. There is a handful of wartime buildings at the Oulton street end, along with a truncated hangar. During Easter 1995, the control tower was extant, but there are reports that it has since been demolished. The memorial on the western edge of Oulton village is easy to miss, it was dedicated on 15th May 1994 to the units that were based.

Of the units that were based at Oulton the most interesting were the three radio counter-measures (RCM) units which flew unsung, but tactically important, deception flights for the USAAF 8th Air Force daylight and RAF Bomber Command night raids. Both the 803rd and 214 Squadron flew the Boeing B-17 Flying Fortress, 223 the Liberator VI. In nearby Blickling Hall (National Trust), there are lists of captains who served with 214 and 223. In the 'Buckingham Arms Hotel' are photographs and a visitors book for RAF aircrew. A book of remembrance is displayed in St Andrews Church.

## SWANNINGTON

6 miles, 15 minutes

*From Oulton, using minor roads, travel through Cawston and Brandiston and south to Swannington.*

Before reaching Swannington, the road unmistakably uses the old perimeter track with a farm track width of a runway remaining. Use the road between Brandiston and Felthorpe for other views. Little remains of the airfield to catalogue, though enough sections of runway and perimeter remain to help visualise the layout. The eastern perimeter track is now the access road to the local church at Stump Cross.

Swannington was a night fighter lair, principally the homes of 85 and 157 Squadrons, both using Mosquitoes. For an airfield with so little for the eye to take in, this is a very rewarding one to visit.

Part of the perimeter track at Swannington (thinned to one section) is now the access road to the church at Stump Cross. Paul Shaw

**Diversion:** Take the minor roads from Swannington through to Felthorpe. South of the village is Felthorpe Aerodrome with a thriving light aircraft population.

## ATTLEBRIDGE
6 miles, 15 minutes

*From Swannington take the minor road to Attlebridge and cross the A1067 heading south west to Weston Longville. The airfield site is south of the village.*

During the Second World War, signposts were removed in order to confuse the enemy, if they were to invade. In the Attlebridge area, these signposts have not been replaced in order to confuse aviation enthusiasts! Directions to find Attlebridge are not easy to give, but the minor roads serve their purpose and the reader's knowledge of airfield layouts will prevail.

Blenheims, Boston and Mitchells formed the early equipment of the units that flew from Attlebridge, then from March 1944 it was the home of the B-24H Liberators of the 466th BG. The village sign is dedicated to the 466th and there is a roll of honour in the parish church. A memorial to the 466th is located at the south west corner of the former airfield, at the junction of two minor roads.

Runways and perimeter track survive, although covered in poultry huts. Few buildings remain, although one blister-type hangar could be found in 1995. Unusually, many of the hard standings at dispersals were still to be seen. Views of runways from the public road are good and while the map shows a footpath crossing the old airfield, there were no signs to identify it.

**To return to Norwich:** Use the A47 and the A1074 to Norwich's inner ring road. Routes to the city centre are well signed and Norwich Airport off the A140 Aylsham and Cromer road.

*Duffy's Tavern*, a Consolidated B-24J Liberator of the 784th Bombardment Squadron, 466th Bombardment Group, in the snow at Attlebridge. via Mike Bailey

**The large memorial to the 466th BG at Attlebridge, dedicated on 12th June 1992.** Paul Shaw

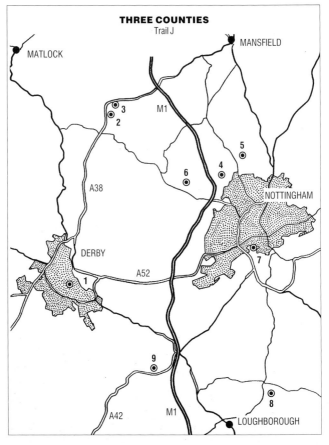

**THREE COUNTIES**
Trail J

1  Derby Industrial Museum
2  Ripley
3  Swanwick
4  Hucknall
5  Papplewick
6  Watnall
7  Nottingham Castle
8  Wymeswold
9  East Midlands Airport

This trail gave me great pleasure to research, because of the different nature of the surprises I found. It also brought home to me the breadth of our aviation heritage. Within the area of this trail are many historical attractions, all worthy of extending your trail. I have not mentioned them all, but one has strong aeronautical associations. This is Hardwick Hall, west of Mansfield and the very first Parachute Regiment camp. (More from the East Midlands Tourism on 01522 531521.)

The Industrial Museum in Derby was a memorable visit. There are few boys who have not had an interest in locomotives and mine was rekindled with a fully fitted cab of a modern engine, all controls to hand and a film running through the windscreen of our progress down the mainline, complete with a soundtrack. A magical moment! With a history of the city's involvement in railways, Crown Derby china, a geological look at the area and the aero engines, all makes this an excellent venue. The RB.211 turbofan is awesome – the feel of power from this giant left me wondering how they ever stop such engines from tearing the wing from the fuselage of giant airliners.

## DERBY

The Industrial Museum, at the Silk Mill, is in the city centre. There is limited parking, but Derby does have a park and ride system. Derby is the home of Rolls-Royce aero engines and here is the largest collection under a single roof. As well as the engines, displays chart the company history. Also within the museum are displays on pottery, minerals and railways. (More details from the museum on 01332 55308 or Derby Tourist Information on 01332 255802.)

**Diversion:** The Coventry Branch of the Rolls-Royce Heritage Trust established themselves in the Rolls-Royce Training School at Mickleover after the factory at Parkside, Coventry, closed in 1994. Here is a superb collection of engines from Armstrong Siddeley and Bristol Siddeley. There is an annual open day, otherwise by prior appointment: RRHT Coventry Branch, Ansty, Coventry, CV7 9JR.

**A small portion of the Rolls-Royce engine hall within the Derby Industrial Museum.** Ken Ellis

## RIPLEY

10 miles, 17 minutes

*From Derby city centre follow signs for the A38, Alfreton, and join this. At the crossing with the B6179 at Holbrook, take the B6179 into Ripley. In the town centre, just after the junction with the B6441, Cromer House is on the left.*

Cromer House, 43 Butterley Hill, Ripley was the birthplace of Barnes Wallis on 26th September 1887. A plaque on the wall commemorates this.

## SWANWICK

1 mile, 6 minutes

*Continue on the B6179, past the Midland Railway Centre. Just before the dual carriageway, turn right into Hickton Road. Towards the far end is a conference centre.*

Although no trace of the wartime use of the Hayes Conference Centre has survived, it has a fascinating past. During the Second World War it was used by the War Office as a prisoner of war camp for German officers. Known as Camp 13, it was requisitioned by September 1940. Five of the occupants lost little time in organising an escape. Just like their counterparts in occupied Europe the methods and problems were the same – hiding the soil, disguising the tunnel, creating air ducts and escape plans once 'beyond the wire'. Of the five, one was to pose as a Dutch pilot involved in secret testing work. His aircraft had force-landed and he was trying to get back to Dyce, in Scotland. They broke out on 20th December 1940.

The man posing as the Dutch pilot was Franz von Werra. Complete in partial flying gear, he made his way to a nearby railway station at Codnor. The station master called the police and the nearest aerodrome, which was Hucknall. At Hucknall, while his story was being checked, von Werra made good his exit through a toilet window. Unknown to him, this put him in the Rolls-Royce side of the airfield. He signed for a Hurricane, had a parachute issued to him and got as far as sitting in the cockpit while waiting for a fitter to fetch a 'trolley ack'. He was arrested – as were the others – who made it as far as Sheffield and Manchester.

Von Werra, of course, went on to become the only German to make a 'home run' from British and Dominion territory and the book The One That Got Away is good reading. He jumped from a train in Canada when he was being transferred. He crossed the frozen St Lawrence river and entered the then neutral USA. There were many diplomatic wrangles, but he got back to Germany, via Latin America. He disappeared over the Dutch coast in 1941, after engine failure.

## HUCKNALL

12 miles, 23 minutes

*Continue on up Hayes Lane, and turn right towards Somercotes, Turn right on the B600 for Selston. Just before Watnall, turn left on the B6009 to Hucknall.*

Rolls-Royce still occupy part of Hucknall, although they no longer use it for flight test and the long north east-south west runway has engine test cells on it. South of this runway can be found the two runways used at weekends by the flying club. The entrance to

The world's first pure jet transport aircraft, the Vickers Type 618 Nene-Viking was tested at Hucknall in 1948-49. A re-engined version of the Viking twin piston engined airliner, the aircraft first flew on 6th April 1948 at Wisley and was involved in a series of tests, both in engine control and helping to pioneer the jet engine into the world of civil aviation. Rolls-Royce

The entrance to the former RAF Hucknall, with the guardroom on the right. Beyond that can be seen the brick door 'runners' for one of the First World War hangars. Paul Shaw

what was RAF Hucknall is off the A6009, close to the 'Will Scarlett' public house. The hangars are now used for warehousing and many former RAF buildings serve light industry and the guardroom serves as a vehicle servicing and parts centre. The number of surviving buildings helps to retain the period 'feel'. Hucknall dates back to the First World War and was expanded in the late 1920s. Rolls-Royce moved in during 1934 and have maintained a presence ever since.

## PAPPLEWICK
7 miles, 16 minutes

*DIVERSION: Leave Hucknall airfield and head for Hucknall heading north on the A611. Follow signs for Linby and stay on the B6011 after the village.*

Papplewick Moor was established as a relief landing ground for Hucknall in 1918, but it saw little use. It was revived again for similar used by Tiger Moths from Hucknall from 1940, but may only have been used for practise approaches and forced-landings, as there were few – if any – facilities on the ground. It was located west of the B683 and south of the B6011, at the junction of the B683 turn right, heading south for Bestwood, and the site of the airfield is on the left.

Continue towards Bestwood and signs for the Model Aviation Centre will be seen, at Goosdale Farm, Moor Road. From models built by special effects companies for film work to a huge 1/7th scale Lancaster, this fascinating place has a large number of models distinguishable from the real thing only by their size. Flying displays are staged most weekends. (More details on 0115 9632175 or Nottingham Tourist Information on 0115 9470661.)

Small selection of the flying models on show at **Papplewick.** Paul Shaw

(Continue to Bestwood, past the Bestwood Country Park and join the A611 towards Hucknall, then back on the tour.)

## WATNALL
2 miles, 6 minutes

*Retrace the route to the junction on the A600, turn left for Nottingham (A610).*

Shortly after the turn, can be seen a goods vehicle testing station. To the right of the testing building is a grass-covered mound with trees on it. This marks the site of the former operations room of 12 Group, Fighter Command. Buried 30ft underground, this was the nerve centre of Britain's aerial defence of the Midlands.

## NOTTINGHAM
6 miles, 19 minutes

Take the A610 into Nottingham. Street parking near the castle is possible on a Sunday and car parks are nearby. On other days, there is a park and ride service.

Within the grounds of the Castle is a statue in memory of Albert Ball VC, a Nottingham lad who became an 'ace' of the Great War with 44 victories, yet lost his life on 7th May 1917, aged 20. There is a small display of Albert Ball artefacts in the castle museum, just outside the Sherwood Foresters Regimental Museum. Despite the size of the display, its impact is enormous. It has Ball's Royal Aero Club flying licence (No 1898) awarded on 15th October 1915, a bullet-shattered windshield carrying the Avro logo, part of a letter to his parents in August 1916

**Now a vehicle testing station, the mound of earth and trees denote what was the underground operations room of 12 Group.** Paul Shaw

**Display of Albert Ball artefacts in Nottingham Castle.** Paul Shaw

detailing a combat with 14 of the enemy, 15 miles over the lines and others. There is an air intake pipe from his Nieuport 17, along with an account of an action where he only just made it back over his own lines through lack of fuel. There is also a German message canister, with streamer, of the type used to confirm to the Royal Flying Corps that Albert Ball had been killed in action. (Details of castle entry, admission etc on 0115 9483504, or Nottingham Tourist Centre on 0115 9470661.

**Statue in memory of Albert Ball vc in the grounds of Nottingham castle.** Paul Shaw

## WYMESWOLD

15 miles, 30 minutes

*Leave Nottingham to the south, signs vary, and pick up the A60 for Rempstone and Barrow upon Soar. In Hoton, turn left for Wymeswold.*

Wymeswold has much to see, predominantly on the technical site. The airfield is largely on private land, but there are plenty of gateways for viewing, including the runway. Two runways and substantial sections of perimeter track are extant. The control tower is derelict. There is one 'B1' hangar and three 'T2s', one of which is used as a go-kart circuit and is open to the public. The water tower still stands and dominates the many

Fire tender house extant at Wymeswold.

The water tower dominating a 'T2' hangar at Wymeswold. Both Paul Shaw

smaller buildings which survive in conditions ranging from poor to good.

Opened in May 1942, Wymeswold was a bomber training airfield and later come under Transport Command with Douglas Dakotas until 1947. From 1949 it was the home of a variety of units, auxiliary and front-line until the RAF left in 1957. Following this it was used for major airline overhaul work by Fields Aircraft Services until they moved to east Midlands Airport in 1968.

## EAST MIDLANDS AIRPORT
12 miles, 23 minutes

*Follow the A60 north, signed for Nottingham. At Rempstone, turn left on to the A6006 signed for Ashby de la Zouch and East Midlands Airport. At the junction with the A6 turn right for Kegworth. Go through Kegworth and at the junction with the M1, follow the signs to the airport.*

The former Castle Donington airfield, was opened in January 1943 initially as a bomber and then as a transport operational training unit and closed in September 1946. The site was very convenient for the three counties of Derbyshire, Nottinghamshire and Leicestershire who were participating in a scheme to operate an airport. East Midlands Airport opened on 1st April 1965.

There are no features to remind one of its wartime service. Everything is modern and built to serve the needs of today. Until late 1995 there was an excellent visitor centre – the Aeropark – with displays on the history of the airfield and aviation in general. It offered commanding views of the comings and goings while allowing the terminal to be unclut-

tered with spectators. Finally there was a goodly collection of aircraft to view, including a Argosy, Buccaneer, Lightning, Varsity and a Vulcan. In March 1996 it was announced that the 'temporary' closure while freight bay work was undertaken was to become permanent. As this work went to press, there seemed little chance of a reprieve – a sad moment as another pleasing and functional facility is removed from us.

**Diversions:** The Donington Collection of racing cars is just a mile further west on the A453 and located on the racing circuit. (More details on 01332 810048 or Derby Tourist Information on 01332 255802.)

In Coalville is the Snibston Discovery Centre (12 miles, 16 minutes). From the airport, continue on the A453 to the junction with the A42 and join this, signed Ashby de la Zouch. Come off at the junction with the A50 and take this towards Leicester. At the roundabout with the A442, leave the A50 and follow the signs for Snibston.

Here is an excellent museum, based upon a former colliery site, charting Leicestershire's industrial past, present and future. There is a pleasing railway section and a lot of 'hands on' exhibits.

An Auster AOP.9 is displayed to show the county's former aviation industry and a display of the Whittle jet engine, which was developed at Lutterworth. (More details on 01530 510851, Tourist Information Centre on site, 01530 813608.

**To rejoin the trail:** Retrace steps to the junction of the A442 and the A50 and take the A50 towards Leicester. Join the M1 northbound at Junction 22. Pick up the trail options at Junction 24, Kegworth.

**To return to Derby:** From the airport main entrance turn left on the A453 and follow the signs for the A6 Derby. Join the A6 at the junction with the M1. Derby Industrial Museum is in the very centre of the city and is well signed. The museum does have its own car park but spaces are limited. (14 miles, 25 minutes.)

**Alternatively:** From the airport main entrance turn left on the A453 and follow the signs for the M1. Join the M1 northbound and leave at Junction 25, the A52 to Derby.

Just off the A52 in Spondon is the large Courtauld's plant, this is modern and sprawling, but while driving past it is worth pondering its link with aviation. In the early days of aircraft, the frame was covered in linen. In order to prevent the passage of air though the linen, to increase both lift and durability, a dope was applied. This word originates not with the Americanism for a stupefying drink or drug, but from the Dutch *doop*, meaning sauce. Early dopes were low nitrated cellulose which were high inflammable. A dope was developed in Germany of cellulose acetate which was non-inflammable and had the advantage of being tough yet pliable.

When war broke out in 1914, such dope was available to Britain through one Swiss company and one French. By 1915, supplies were becoming difficult and the government invited tenders for the production of 100 tons of cellulose acetate in Britain. Only Dr Dreyfus of the Cellonite Company in Basle replied! Discussions were not successful and it took an approach by private companies to secure an agreement with Dr Dreyfus in 1916 to use his process at Spondon. The first ton of dope passed inspection in April 1917.

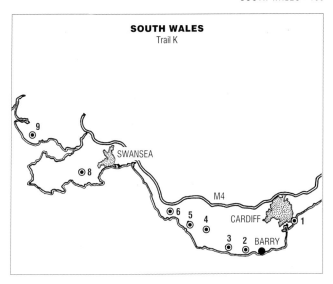

## SOUTH WALES
Trail K

1  Pengam Moor
2  Cardiff-Wales Airport
3  St Athan
4  Llandow
5  St Brides
6  Stormy Down
7  Swansea
8  Swansea Airport
9  Pembrey

For me, South Wales was an enigma. With no major museum, few memorials, no aerodrome preserved in a time warp and no hectic aerial activity. Yet, from seven in the morning until six in the evening, with refreshments taken like a Tornado suckling from a tanker, I was completely and totally absorbed, covering a journey which only needed two and a half hours.

Llandow is a gem, it was wonderful to explore, the kind of place where the obvious is just out of reach. Like a prism, a change of position and the pieces appear randomly scattered. Many of the buildings and hangars can be enjoyed from close up.

I had much to be grateful for the possession of *British Airfield Buildings of the Second World War* by Graham Buchan Innes (see page 125 for details). There were many hangar types that were new to me, and even now, I would hesitate to say I'm spot on. But what would I have made of the dome trainer at Pembrey without it?

I have written of Pengam Moor being fragile, but with the last small section of runway occupying prime building land, hangars sporting 'Unsafe' signs and structures made of wood, I felt that what I saw would not be there much longer. I hope I'm wrong.

## PENGAM MOOR

*From the M4, leave by Junction 29 (if westbound), or Junction 30 (eastbound). Both lead to the A48, leave at the exit for Cardiff East, A4161. This joins the A4232, follow signs Docks and Atlantic Wharf. Before the steel works turn into Seawall Road. At the end, Kenyon Road and Pengam Road can be found.*

This area follows the pattern of urbanisation so strikingly similar to Skellingthorpe (see Trail G) with pockets of aeronautical architecture and ground work extant. The difference is that what remains at Pengam Moor has an air of fragility. Of the three Bellman hangars to be found, one is in use as a warehouse, but the other two displayed warning signs, declaring them unsafe. The hangars reside within a cramped industrial estate behind the steel works. There is not one ounce of aerodrome 'feel' surrounding them, rather an image that they have been brought in from elsewhere.

In Tremorfa Park, off Kenyon Road, the athletic and social club uses wooden buildings of the Air Ministry type. The service roads are clearly those of an airfield and extend around the playing fields. Nearby is the much more substantial, brick built, motor transport section. A short section of runway still survived in early 1996. Access roads were already built and housing work was continuing at a pace.

On Pengam Road is 'The Old Airport' public house, a reminder of the origins of the airfield as Cardiff Airport. (See our sister book *Aeronautical Pubs and Inns of Britain*.) From the former Cardiff Airport, the next destination is the current example.

**Diversion:** The Welsh Industrial and Maritime Museum is to be found north of Butetown on the former Bute 'E' Dock. This is south west of Pengam Moor and well signposted. A excellent collection of artefacts large and small charts Welsh maritime and industrial achievements. A Westland Wessex HAS.1 helicopter is also on show. (More details on 01222 481919.) Cardiff-Wales Airport is signed from the city centre.

Classic Air Ministry wooden hutting at Pengam Moor. Paul Shaw

## CARDIFF-WALES AIRPORT
16 miles, 32 minutes

*Retrace the route from Pengam Moor to the A48. Follow signs for M4 West and City Centre. The route to the airport is well signed off the A48.*

A modern airport with a spectator area on the top floor, offering an excellent view. On the opposite side from the terminal, on the Aircraft Maintenance Facility South, are a Bellman and a Robin hangar. The airfield started life with the local name Rhoose in 1941, it became Cardiff Airport in 1954.

## ST ATHAN
4 miles, 7 minutes

*Take the B4265, signed Llantwit Major, to St Athan. Follow signs for RAF St Athan, and turn left for Boverton. An unsigned right turn to Picketston takes in the remote site.*

St Athan is an enormous maintenance and storage facility for the RAF, all of which is in a secure area. The station is easily circumnavigated by public roads and there is much to take in. During weekdays, there is much activity, with aircraft on air test, or ground-running, plus a selection of types in open storage, or being stripped of spares.

Hangars are dispersed on seven locations and amount to four 'B1's, six Lamellas, three Bellmans, three 'C' types two 'D' types and two modern hangars of huge proportions. The Picketston site is linked to the main airfield by a taxi track that crosses the back road from St Athan to Boverton.

Since its inception in 1939, St Athan has always been a maintenance and storage specialist. In days gone by vast numbers of aircraft were held awaiting issue to service, or the axe.

Currently the base undertakes overhaul work on the following types: BAC VC-10 tanker/transports, BAe Harrier and Hawk, Panavia Tornado, Sepecat Jaguar and others as needs demand. A small school of technical training uses a variety of instructional airframes. A McDonnell Douglas Phantom FGR.2 is displayed within the camp.

## LLANDOW
4 miles, 6 minutes

*Rejoin the B4265 and travel toward Llantwit Major and Bridgend. Turn right at the traffic island on to the B4270, signed Llandow. Brown tourist sign for caravans and the racing circuit lead to the site, but there is much to see further out.*

The former Llandow aerodrome is an aeronautical treasure. Like St Athan, it was largely employed in storage and maintenance. It closed in the late 1950s. All of the hangars are in good condition, much of the runway structure also survives and is used as public road or go-kart track. The perimeter track has fared less well.

The control tower is in good health and occupied by a cafe and estate offices. Close by are the buildings which normally comprise the fire tender shelter, floodlight trailer and tractor shed, crash party hut and night flying equipment store. The water tower still serves the buildings around it, both old and new. Easily recognisable are the headquarters building and the guardroom.

There is a small memorial dedicated to all of the units that operated from Llandow 1941-57. This is not easy to find and is on the way towards Sigingstone.

The hangars are in five locations, comprising three 'K' types and seven Lamellas, many of which are in use, one as a furniture store.

Llandow's greatest attribute is the accessibility afforded because of the varied usage to which the airfield site is now put. The relief of the land, the re-introduction of hedgerows and the nature of the dispersed airfield all conspire to necessitate explorations, and a visit is all the more enjoyable because of its layout and atmosphere.

Memorial to Llandow's units: 614 Squadron, 53 Operational Training Unit, 4 Civilian Anti-Aircraft Co-operation Unit and 38 Maintenance Unit. Beware, it is easy to miss! Paul Shaw

The control tower at Llandow is well preserved and currently houses a couple of offices and the 'Tower Cafe' – well worth a visit.

Guardroom (or Warden's Office) and Lamella at Llandow. The accessibility of the former airfield makes it an airfield buildings enthusiast's delight. Both Paul Shaw

## ST BRIDES
8 miles, 13 minutes

*Rejoin the B4265 to St Bride's Major.*

As might be expected, St Bride's was a 'minimal' airfield used from 1941 as a satellite landing ground for St Athan's 19 Maintenance Unit. Aircraft were stored in the open and ferried to Llandow or St Athan for work and issue to service. It closed in late 1945.

Located half a mile south of the village, inspection in early 1996 found what may have been a guardroom, but no further evidence.

## STORMY DOWN
8 miles, 15 minutes

*Rejoin the B4265, signed Bridgend. At the roundabout in Bridgend, turn left on to the A48 signed Port Talbot. After the A4106 to Porthcawl leaves the A48, after a short distance turn left for Tytheston, at the transmitter mast the site of the old Stormy Down airfield is to the right.*

Two hangars and two hangar bases, a water tower, the machine gun butts and a large area of dereliction easily identify the site of the old airfield. Both of the hangars, an 'F' and a 'VR' type, were in use and in good condition, one serving as an indoor kart track, the other for industry.

Built pre-war, opening in 1939, the station was originally known as Porthcawl, but changed to Stormy Down by 1940. Most of its use was as a gunnery training station, it closed in 1945.

## SWANSEA
10 miles, 25 minutes

*Retrace the route to the A48, and follow signs for Port Talbot, joining the M4 at Junction 37. Leave the M4 at Junction 42, joining the A483 which runs into the city centre.*

There is a stained glass memorial window to 10 group, Fighter Command, in St Mary's Church. (Details from the Swansea Tourist Information Centre on 01792 468321.) The church, with a square tower and castelated top is close to Swansea museum. Alongside the River Tawe bridge in the city centre an anti-aircraft gun is mounted on a brick plinth as a monument.

## SWANSEA AIRPORT
8 miles, 17 minutes

*Take the A4067 seafront road (signed Mumbles) eastwards out of Swansea city centre. Swansea Airport is well signed on the A4118 Gower Road.*

Swansea Airport provides an intimate welcome that is only possible at a small aerodrome. Add to this welcome the provision of food and drink, or just an ice cream. Call this venue the 'Spitfire Bar and Grill' and position it in the ground floor of the wartime control tower. Set up picnic tables outside, offering excellent views of the aerodrome, including winch-launching of Viking gliders of 636 Volunteer Gliding School. Result, a perfect place to linger.

Known initially as Fairwood Common, from its place on the Gower Peninsula, the airfield thundered to the sounds of Spitfires,

**Well-maintained hangar at Stormy Down.** Paul Shaw

**The wartime tower still serves its original role at present day Swansea Airport, although it has been much-modified.** Ken Ellis

Hurricanes and Mosquitoes among others during the Second World War. The traditional three runway pattern is still used, although two have been truncated. Travelling down the A4118 passed the entrance to the aerodrome, extant sections of what would be today's runways 28 and 33 can be found on the 'wrong' side of the road. There are two hangars and many of the small buildings are clearly all Air Ministry pattern, including some wooden huts.

## PEMBREY
20 miles, 37 minutes

*Retrace the route along the A4118 towards Swansea. Take the B4296 to Gowertown and then follow the signs for Llanelli, turning left on to the A484. Continue on the A484 through and out of Llanelli (signed Carmarthen) and at Pembrey follow brown tourist signs for the country park and race circuit.*

There are two derelict 'VR' type hangars and a smaller number of wartime buildings surviving at Pembrey. Most famous of the extant buildings is a dome trainer, a very rare survivor. A runway is used as part of a motor racing track. The airfield's longest resident during the war was 1 Air Gunnery School, taking advantage of the ranges to the north of Pembrey Forest – which are still 'live'.

Munitions have played a large part in the area's history. Close to the former airfield is Pembrey Country Park which offers a wide range of distractions, including a narrow gauge railway. What makes the park unique is that the area was formerly a Royal Ordnance Factory. Old storage bunkers of all sizes can be found all over the park. The narrow gauge railway uses the track of the old storage depot line.

**To return to the M4, Junction M4:** Retrace the route along the A484 to Llanelli, and follow signs for the M4. (67 miles, 70 minutes)

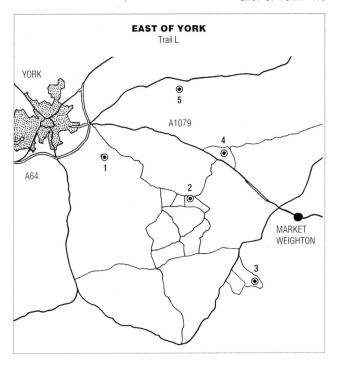

**EAST OF YORK**
Trail L

YORK

A1079

A64

MARKET
WEIGHTON

1 Elvington
2 Melbourne
3 Holme-on-Spalding Moor
4 Pocklington
5 Full Sutton

Smaller at first sight, there may look less on this trail, but there is so much to see, it would be overkill to encourage you to see more. When I set off exploring on this trail, I had hopes and aspirations for what I might find. The Yorkshire Air Museum is a venue I have and will again visit, time after time. It is the engineer in me that enjoys the progress of restoration as it allows an insight into the mechanics under the gloss of a finished product. Allied to this are the excellent displays and the ever enjoyable restaurant/NAAFI. Also on route, always a source of great joy, a pub with an aviation provenance. Many wartime hangars and smaller buildings, memorials in stone and glass, airfields from where men rose to great deeds.

This trail did fulfil my aspirations, and though the ingredients are available everywhere, it seems that here in Yorkshire, they are blended in the right quantities and with the right amount of passion.

## ELVINGTON

*From the A64 York bypass, take the exit signed Hull, the A1079, then immediate right on the B1228, signed Elvington. Between here and the museum, look out for the memorial which marks the site where a German aircraft crashed.*

Home of the Yorkshire Air Museum. The major project here is the recreation of a Handley Page Halifax, always a source of interest no matter what the stage of progress. A 'T2' hangar has been brought onto site and will be completed during 1996, whereupon the Halifax will be moved in and progress on restoration is expected to be rapid. There is another restoration project here, a Mosquito NF.II being undertaken by the Night Fighter Preservation Team.

Pride of place in the buildings is the control tower, full restored and kitted out, this building is charged with atmosphere. There are exhibitions devoted to Gus Walker, Barnes Wallis, the Royal Observer Corps, Air Gunners Association and there is an extensive archive section. Along with many other exhibits are the airframes. These include a Gloster Meteor F.8, English Electric Canberra T.4 and Lightning F.6, Handley Page Victor K.2, Hawker Hunter T.7, Hawker Siddeley Buccaneer S.2 and others. The museum-run 'NAAFI' is in a period building, and the food is well recommended.

As well as a touching memorial rose garden, dedicated to 4 and 6 Groups RCAF, there is a memorial to 77 Squadron which flew Halifaxes from Elvington 1942-44. (More details of the Yorkshire Air Museum on 01904 608595, or York Tourist Information on 01904 620557.)

The airfield was operational until recently as a satellite landing ground for Linton-on-Ouse with a modern runway and an enormous apron, said to be visible from space. The runway was extended to 9,800ft and the aprons built in anticipation of the airfield being used by the USAF in the mid-1950s. The Americans used the facilities for only a brief time.

Leave the Yorkshire Air Museum by turning right on to the B1228 to Elvington. In only a quarter of a mile on the right is the memorial to the Free French Air Force Halifax Squadrons based at Elvington as part of the *Groupes Lourds* ('Heavy' Groups). Nos 346 *Guyenne* and 347 *Tunisie* were both based during 1944-45 The memorial stands back from the road and may be easily missed.

The buildings within the Yorkshire Air Museum generate lots of atmosphere – the NAAFI is a great attraction. Ken Ellis

Memorial to 77 Squadron, who flew Halifax IIs and Vs out of Elvington from October 1942 to May 1944. Paul Shaw

New exhibit for the Yorkshire Air Museum is Meteor F.8 WL168, previously the 'gate guardian' at the now closed RAF Finningley. Alan Curry

Memorial to Elvington's French bomber units in the village includes a cut-out outline of a Halifax. Paul Shaw

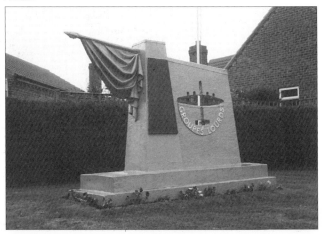

## MELBOURNE
8 miles, 15 minutes

*Continue and follow the B1228 until it follows a turning on the right, shortly after crossing the Pocklington Canal. Do not follow the B1228, carry straight on for Melbourne. On passing the Cross Keys public house, take the next right turn for Seaton Ross. At the next crossroads, give way and turn left for Seaton Ross. The Melbourne memorial to 10 Squadron is on the right along this road.*

This airfield is in private hands and does not lend itself to be seen by the public. The runways and perimeter track are extant along with a B1 hangar. The hangar can be easily seen from the public road. There is a memorial here to 10 Squadron, who flew Halifaxes from here 1942-45. A few small wartime buildings can also be seen from the road.

An old favourite haunt of Melbourne airmen was the public house in nearby Seaton Ross, to the south of the former airfield. Always known as 'The Bombers', it was in fact 'The Blacksmiths Arms'. The nickname has never gone away and just recently, the name has been officially changed to 'Bombers Inn'. The pub sign outside shows three Halifax in a vic formation carrying the 10 Squadron codes 'ZA-'. The door knocker is the 10 Squadron badge. One room of the pub is called 10 Squadron lounge and the walls are covered in framed photographs of the unit, recalling some of its history. No.10 Squadron Association who meet at the pub once a month. The bar front in the bar room

Hallowed meeting place and 'living' memorial to 10 Squadron, 'Bombers Inn' at Seaton Ross.
Paul Shaw

**Memorial to 10 Squadron at Melbourne.**
Paul Shaw

came from the Officers Mess of RAF Melbourne following a fire there. A plaque against the doorway records this and that it is claimed the timber came from York Minister. Note that 'The Bombers' is not open at lunch times during the weekdays, more details on 01759 318781.

## HOLME-ON-SPALDING MOOR
6 miles, 13 minutes

*Turn left from 'The Bombers' car park signed for Howden and Selby and continue through the village by the church. At the junction with the A163, turn left for Holme-on-Spalding Moor. At the junction of the A163 and A614 in Holme, turn right for Goole on the A614. In only a little distance, turn left at the sign for Land of Nod and Holme Industrial Estate.*

The use of this airfield by Blackburn and British Aerospace after the war, has meant that many buildings have survived. So many in fact, that it is wonderful to see them. They include the battle headquarters, parachute store, motor transport section, guardroom and so many of the utilities, even latrines. One 'J' type hangar remains unchanged. The two 'T2' hangars have been joined, their gantries and doors removed and modern cladding fitted to complete a disguise. Only the roof line and external dimensions remain to bear witness to their former identity. Buildings range from poor to excellent in terms of upkeep and their type of use has not spoilt the feel of an airfield here.

Runways and perimeter track have been removed except for a long farm track width on one runway. On the opposite side of the airfield from the industrial estate, there is only a taxi track in front of a farmhouse and a culvert which carried a runway over a drainage ditch.

Just inside the gateway are the memorials, one in stone to remember personnel of 76 Squadron who gave their lives in the cause of freedom. A memorial tree has been planted alongside in memory of these members of number 458 (RAAF) Squadron, who gave their lives. Just behind is another tree in commemoration of the life of Group Captain Lord Cheshire VC, OM, DSO, DFC, 1917-92 who was commanding officer of 76 Squadron from 1942-43.

Retrace the route to the A614 and turn right, then turn right for the A163 signed Bridlington. On the outskirts of the village, there is a hidden track up to the parish church of All Saints and a footpath from alongside the garage. There is a memorial window to 76 Squadron and the airmen's graves are towards the back of the churchyard.

Most Buccaneers made the first flights from Holme-on-Spalding Moor, having been assembled at Brough. The third S.2, XN976, was used for trials with the Martin Bullpup air-to-surface missile from Holme in 1965. BAe

Refurbished and updated parachute store still in use at Holme-on-Spalding Moor. Paul Shaw

**Memorial to 76 Squadron inside the entrance to Holme-on-Spalding Moor.** Paul Shaw

## POCKLINGTON
9 miles, 15 minutes

*Continue along the A163, signed Great Driffield and Bridlington. Turn left on to the A1079, signed York, ignore signs for Pocklington, follow signs for Pocklington Industrial Estate.*

Pocklington aerodrome retains its title by virtue of it being the home of the Wolds Gliding Club. Many buildings remain in good condition along with four hangars, one 'J' type, two 'T2s' and one 'B1'. Not obvious at first sight, the 'B1' doors and gantries are still in situ on the rear elevation. Two runways remain in reasonable condition and section of perimeter track remains in poor condition.

The technical site has become an industrial estate with wartime buildings scattered within, although there is a cluster of old buildings in good condition which seem to have formed a redoubt against progress. Views over the airfield are unimpeded and can be enjoyed from public roads on a circular route.

The gliding club can be reached from the A1079 and is the turn after that for the industrial estate. In front of the gliding club is a memorial to 102 and 405 Squadrons who operated Halifaxes from RAF Pocklington.

## FULL SUTTON
6 miles, 15 minutes

*Continue toward Pocklington from the Wolds Gliding Club and in Pocklington turn left for Stamford Bridge. Continue through Fangfoss and turn left at the sign for Full Sutton Industrial Estate and the old aerodrome. To the right at this crossroads is an old accommodation site.*

Full Sutton has not fared as well as the other airfields on the tour. Whilst it has retained two hangars and many buildings, a grain store has spoilt the atmosphere of the area. On the plus side, many buildings are still in use with little alteration to looks and situation, the control tower is in good condition

**The control tower at Full Sutton in November 1995, used as offices.** Paul Shaw

and in use as offices, the two hangars are used within a second-hand parts business and the main road of the industrial estate is the perimeter track. Only a short section of one runway remains and the airfield is used by light aircraft.

**To return to Elvington:** From the old aerodrome drive, turn left for Full Sutton then turn for York on the A166. When at the A64 (York bypass) instructions as given under Elvington, above. (12 miles, 25 minutes)

## LOCATION INDEX

We hope you have enjoyed this Midland Publishing book. Our titles are carefully edited and designed for you by knowledgeable and enthusiastic specialists, with over 20 years of experience. Further titles are in the course of preparation but we would welcome ideas on what you would like to see. If you have a manuscript or project that requires publishing, we should be happy to consider it; brief details initially please.

In addition, our associate company, Midland Counties Publications, offers an exceptionally wide range of aviation, astronomy, military and railway books/videos for sale by mail-order around the world. For a copy of the appropriate catalogue, please write, telephone or fax to:
Midland Counties Publications
Unit 3 Maizefield, Hinckley Fields, Hinckley, Leics, LE10 1YF
Tel: 01455 233747; Fax: 01455 841805

## WRECKS & RELICS
## 15th Edition

Ken Ellis

*Wrecks & Relics* has been a cherished part of the world of aviation heritage since the first edition was published 35 years ago. The 15th edition, expanded and refined, will be much sought after by enthusiasts in the UK and Ireland.

The book lists and traces the movements of thousands of aircraft held in museums, preserved with individuals, in use as gate guardians, instructional airframes, on fire dumps etc, in the United Kingdom and Ireland, and on RAF bases overseas.

Includes museums with opening times, BAPC member groups, BAPC/IAHC registers, and enormously useful indexes by both aircraft type and location. New for this edition is an examination of export aircraft, still further improved layout for even easier reference and an expanded photographs section.

**Previous editions still in print:**
12th edition (1990) 252pp
**£9.95**
14th edition (1994) 336pp      **£12.95**

Laminated Hardback
210 x 148 mm, 350 pages
with about 200 photos.
1 85780 047 8   May
**£14.95**

**BRITISH AIRFIELD
BUILDINGS OF WWII**
Aviation Pocket Guide 1

Graham Buchan Innes

The world of airfield buildings is one
of constant fascination to enthusiasts.
Until now, references on this subject
have been the domain of very
specialist works, or to be partially
found within high price books. All of
this has conspired to put off a whole
army of people who have a thirst for
such knowledge.

*British Airfield Buildings* is the
answer to this need and in a
genuinely pocket-size form. From
control towers, to hangars, to
defensive strongpoints, barrack
blocks, maintenance buildings to the
humble latrine, it provides an
illustration of a *surviving* example,
highlighting details and other styles
of similar building.

Over 200 illustrations with brief but
informative captions take the reader
for an excursion through a typical
wartime station.

*British Airfield Buildings* provides
an ideal primer to a subject close to
the heart of all enthusiasts.

Softback
148 x 105 mm, 128 pages
230 b/w photographs
1 85780 026 5   Available
**£5.95**

## AVIATION MUSEUMS OF BRITAIN
Aviation Pocket Guide 2

Ken Ellis

All aviation enthusiasts look forward
to visiting an aviation museum and
often plan their journeys to make sure
that one (or more!) can be taken in.
*Aviation Museums of Britain* provides
the important information that most
people need to know before setting
out: When is it open? Which ones are
open off-season? Is there a cafe? Is
there somewhere for the kids to play?
Is there a shop to browse around?
This book answers all of these
questions and of course provides an
easy-to-read review of what aircraft
exhibits are on show and a
breakdown of other displays, features
and themes within Britain's 80
aviation museums.

The book goes much further in
helping the reader plan a full day – or
weekend – away with suggestions of
other attractions nearby, allowing *all*
of the family to find something of
interest.

An invaluable guide, opening up
many ideas and possibilities.
A constant companion in the glove
box or the pocket.

Softback
148 x 105mm, 128 pages
112 b/w photographs
1 85780 038 X   Available
**£5.95**

## AERONAUTICAL PUBS & INNS OF BRITAIN
Aviation Pocket Guide 3

Dave Smith with Ken Ellis

There can be few more perfect combinations than aircraft and pubs. Aviation enthusiasts all over the UK have a passion for both. An amazing number of public houses and inns have strong aeronautical connections.

The *Air Balloon* at Birdlip was a venue for Edwardian ballooning adventurès; the *Sir Frank Whittle* in Lutterworth is close to where the first British jet engine ran; the *Bader Arms* was opened by the famous Battle of Britain fighter pilot; and the *Double O Two* near Bristol celebrates the first British-built Concorde.

There is a great fascination in these inns, their signs and their significance, but this book also takes the interest into a much overlooked area – watering holes. All major bomber and fighter stations had favourite places for their airmen to go and unwind.

Topping off a fascinating study is a look at the growing number of aircraft to be found adorning night clubs! A gazetteer of existing aeronautical pubs and inns completes this absorbing guide.

Softback
148 x 105 mm, c80 pages
B/w and colour photos
1 85780 048 6   May
**£5.95**

# FlyPast

**B**ritain's top-selling aviation monthly has a very special place in the hearts of enthusiasts all over the world.

Through the years, readers have come

*...FlyPast the journal that leads in the fascinating world of aviation history...*

to regard *FlyPast* as the magazine covering the world of aviation history, especially its coverage of *living* history. *FlyPast* has never contented itself with just monitoring news of aircraft and events worldwide as they happen, its editorial staff and a network of renowned contributors have built up a reputation as news and opinion makers in their own right. All of this combines to make *FlyPast* the journal that *leads* in the fascinating world of aviation history, museums, displays, operators and aircraft. Don't stand on the touch-lines, *take part* with *FlyPast!*

Monthly

### Free Membership

In addition, as a subscriber you'll become an automatic member of the

*FlyPast* club. This exclusive club was launched to offer its members fantastic benefits. There's a regular newsletter, special privileges, club discounts on selected items, museum visits, lectures and much, much more.

To ensure you never miss an issue of *FlyPast* place a regular order with your newsagent or take out a post-free postal subscription. See the current issue of *FlyPast* for rates or contact:- Subscription Dept., Key Publishing Ltd., PO Box 100, Stamford, Lincs., PE9 1XQ. Tel:- 01780 55131, Fax:- 01780 57261 or EMail:- subs@keymags.demon.co.uk.

# FlyPast

**Full of Facts, Full of Memories**